LANGUAGE AND LITERACY SERIES

Dorothy S. Strickland, FOUNDING EDITOR
Celia Genishi and Donna E. Alvermann, SERIES EDITORS

(continued)

Race, Community, and Urban Schools

Partnering with African American Families

STUART GREENE

Foreword by Patricia A. Edwards

Teachers College, Columbia University
New York and London

Published by Teachers College Press, 1234 Amsterdam Avenue, New York, NY 10027

Chapter 2 is based on S. Greene (2013). Mapping Low-Income African American Parents' Roles in Their Children's Education in a Changing Political Economy. *Teachers College Record, 115*(10).

Library of Congress Cataloging-in-Publication Data

Greene, Stuart.
　　Race, community, and urban schools : partnering with African American
　　　　families / Stuart Greene ; foreword by Patricia Edwards.
　　　　　　pages cm. — (Language and literacy series)
　　Includes bibliographical references and index.
　　ISBN 978-0-8077-5464-1 (pbk. : alk. paper)
　　ISBN 978-0-8077-5465-8 (hardcover : alk. paper)
　　　　1. African American children—Education—Case studies. 2. Education—
　　Parent participation—United States—Case studies. 3. Education, Urban—
　　United States—Case studies. 4. Community and school—United States—
　　Case studies. I. Title.
　　LC2717.G728　2013
　　371.829'96073—dc23　　　　　　　　　　　　　　　　　　2013021450

ISBN 978-0-8077-5464-1 (paper)
ISBN 978-0-8077-5465-8 (hardcover)

Printed on acid-free paper
Manufactured in the United States of America

20　19　18　17　16　15　14　13　　　　　8　7　6　5　4　3　2　1

Contents

Foreword

Thirty years ago, the highly acclaimed National Commission on Excellence in Education's celebrated report *A Nation at Risk* (1983) had a strong message for all families, including African American families. The Commission noted:

> You bear a responsibility to participate actively in your child's education. You should encourage more diligent study and discourage satisfaction with mediocrity and the attitude that says "let it slide"; monitor your child's study; encourage good study habits; encourage your child to take more demanding rather than less demanding courses; nurture your child's curiosity, creativity, and confidence; and be an active participant in the work of the schools. (p. 35)

This message reminded me of a time during my childhood when parent involvement was an integral part of a successful schooling experience for students. By participating in various activities and supporting the school's literacy curriculum, parents showed their children that they valued education. I met many poor Black parents who were not middle-class, but as Sampson (2004) correctly noted, "some poor blacks . . . appear to be middle class and do many of the things that seem to be important for good academic performance for their children" (p. 12). Similarly, I met parents like those whom Lareau (2000) described. She found that non-mainstream parents who lack knowledge do not necessarily lack interest in their children's schools or in learning how to help their children.

My mother was president of the PTA throughout my 6 years of elementary school, which meant that my sister and I had to attend all of the PTA meetings. In fact, we provided the entertainment at these monthly meetings, as we offered musical selections on the piano and xylophone. We also assisted Mama with fundraising activities. As I reflect back on these PTA meetings, I can remember hearing my mama telling parents: "Education is the key to a better life and brighter future for our children. We, as parents, must help the teachers help our children in school. We want our children to have a better life than we have right now."

My mother believed like I do, that every parent and child has strengths. As a young child growing up in the Deep South in the 1950s and 1960s, I often heard adults make comments like those made by Epps, Clark, and Jackson. Epps noted that "the family is the basic institution through which children learn who they are, where they fit into society, and what kinds of futures they are likely to experience" (1983, p. ix). Clark argued, "It is not class position that determines a family's ability to support their children's learning, rather it is the quality of life within the home that makes the difference" (1983, p. xiii). Jesse Jackson (1983) stated, "Parents must make room in their hearts and then in their house and then in their schedule for their children. No poor parent is too poor to do that, and no middle-class parent is too busy." Lastly, but more importantly, I grew up understanding that "Literacy and education are valued possessions that African American families have respected, revered, and sought as a means to personal freedom and communal hope, from enslavement to the present" (Gadsden, 1993, p. 352).

I believe the ultimate expression of education is the partnerships teachers and administrators develop with families, since they prepare students to live in an increasingly diverse world. It is difficult to find a more authentic approach to learning than actual experience. As Dewey expressed in his famous *My Pedagogical Creed*: "education, therefore, is a process of living and not a preparation for future living" (see Archambault, 1964, p. 430). In other words, the efforts that schools make to develop collaborations between home and school should engage families and students in lived experiences that are not a preparation for democratic involvement but are themselves transformative and educative. This process can best be achieved through involvement, partnerships, or collaborations.

Race, Community, and Urban Schools: Partnering with African American Families will make a difference in the lives of teachers and administrators. As you read this book, you may find yourself moved, intrigued, or saddened by some of the examples Stuart Greene provides. And throughout, you will find yourself rethinking, reprocessing, and recreating some of your most cherished ideas or preconceived notions about African American families. It is my hope that this will be your experience because it is precisely the intention of this elegant book.

—Patricia A. Edwards,
Michigan State University; Member, Reading Hall of Fame;
President, International Reading Association, 2010–2011;
Past President, Literacy Research Association
(formerly the National Reading Conference)

Acknowledgments

I would like to thank first the Education Collaborative Group (ECG), which brought together faculty, educators, and community members for a sustained conversation about educational issues for over 2 years. The ECG inspired the work that I did at Ida B. Wells Primary Center and the research that I describe throughout *Race, Community, and Urban Schools*. In particular, I'd like to thank Mary Beckman, associate director for Academic Affairs and Research at the Center for Social Concerns at Notre Dame, who has helped me understand what it means to do community-based research; Jay Caponigro, director of Community Engagement at Notre Dame, from whom I have gained much insight into ways to bring about change; Jennifer Warlick, a professor of economic policy at Notre Dame, who has always challenged me to think rigorously about issues surrounding poverty and education; Joyce Long, my collaborator whose initiatives have made an impact on children and families; Angie Buysse, principal, whose generosity helped sustain the ECG; and Darice Austin Phillips, principal, whose leadership has been both inspiring and transformative.

During these last few years, I have benefited from my friendships with Ronnie, Darryl, Myra, Kenny, and LaQuisha. They humbled me with their stories of extraordinary perseverance, integrity, and insights about people. They are their children's first teachers. They were my teachers as well, and I hope I have given their stories justice here.

I have also benefited a great deal from a number of colleagues and friends in the Education, Schooling, and Society program at Notre Dame, especially Julie Turner, a professor of psychology who served as a member of the ECG and who I consider a valued mentor and guide. Nancy McAdams, Maria McKenna, Kevin Burke, Jim Frabutt, and Brian Collier have offered generous and kind responses to my work. Thanks as well to Peter Smagorinsky, Latrise Johnson, and Valerie Kinloch for reading and responding thoughtfully to my writing. I especially appreciate the grants from the Institute for Scholarship in the Liberal Arts at Notre Dame to support my research and the sabbatical I received from the College of Arts and Letters. I owe a debt of gratitude to Megan White, Philip Langthorne, and Martin Gallagher for coordinating the efforts of a very able team of undergraduate researchers.

As always, I have enjoyed working with the editors at Teachers College Press. Meg Lemke offered much encouragement during the early stages of this project. I am especially grateful to Emily Spangler, who provided careful readings of my work, kept me on task, and offered valuable suggestions.

Finally, I dedicate *Race, Community, and Urban Schools* to Denise. I have rehearsed the ideas in this book when we hiked in the backcountry of Montana, cycled around Crater Lake, walked the aisles to get groceries, and weeded in the garden. I thank Denise for her enormous patience, support, and devotion. Of course, I know what "paybacks" are like.

Introduction

AUTHOR: How do your parents help you with school activities?

PAIGE: When I have something like homework and it's really hard for me, I ask my mom because she's really good at history. She studies my list and she tells me about what happened in the 1900s and stuff. My mom doesn't know math, my dad does. He knows everything about math.

AUTHOR: Do your parents ever read to you?

PAIGE: Like every time I get ready to go to sleep, my mom, she'll come and read me one of her books.

AUTHOR: How do you feel when your parents read to you, if your mom reads to you?

PAIGE: I feel happy because sometimes I don't like reading because when I'm real sleepy, I'll just let my mom read. She's reading this book, it's called *Raising a Dragon* and it's a good book. She found like a dragon. It was a dragon and there was still a baby dragon inside of it and she heard a loud crack from the cave that she was in and she put on her house shoes and she went to the cave; it's under a waterfall and she brought back the baby dinosaur. She carried her back.

Children's reflections provide a window into the salient moments that define the relationships children have with their families and their worlds of reading. A 4th-grader at the time that I first got to know her, Paige described the roles that her parents played in supporting her schoolwork at home. They monitored her work when she returned home from school, helped her when she had difficulty learning new subjects, provided encouragement when she shared her tests with them, and played very active roles in fostering her sense of curiosity, love of learning, and confidence. Reading to Paige at bedtime, her mother also conveyed a sense of emotional warmth and closeness that nurtured Paige and provided much-needed security and a sense of belonging that the scene of domesticity in *Raising a Dragon* seemed to reinforce. Together, Paige and her mother often visited the library and Paige recalled a time when "[her mother] just got on the computer and just started looking up stuff for me to read and then I just started reading." Thus her mother reaffirmed Paige's identity as a reader, the social nature of learning, and the joy of "just looking up stuff." (All names throughout are pseudonyms.)

Children's lives evolve and change over time. It is important to capture these changes to fully grasp both children's development and the nature of their families' involvement (e.g., Compton-Lilly, 2007). In a conversation a year later, Paige again describes her enthusiasm for reading, but explains that, as a 5th-grader, she is becoming more independent:

> Author: Do your parents read to you?
> Paige: Sometimes . . . I like to read by myself.
> Author: What do you like to read?
> Paige: One of my favorite books is a Bluford High book called *The Test* and another Bluford High book called *Pretty Ugly*.

Her parents created the expectation that Paige become a reader and develop a literate identity. Paige also relied on her family for the kinds of "guidance, skills, and values" that Comer (2004) described as essential to children's "social functioning and self-expression" (p. 57).

I have also gotten to know Jada, a 5th-grader who, like Paige, loved to read. Sometimes she read with her mother and her aunt, while at other times she spent time with her younger cousin with whom she lived:

> I read, like sometimes I read my chapter books that I have and 'cause we have a lot of books and so I'll just read to my cousin. Like me and my cousin, we play school a lot, so I'll just read to her or she'll be the teacher and she'll read to me and do work.

In her description, Jada reaffirmed a long-held belief that literacy provides a medium through which to build relationships. Moreover, Jada challenged the assumption that low-income families do not surround children with language-rich environments.

Jada and her cousin often sought out quiet nooks in their modest house, and they squeezed themselves tightly in a closet with just a flashlight. In this quiet space, Jada could imagine a world apart from the day-to-day experiences in school where she felt the pressures of increased testing and the disinvested spaces of an unsafe neighborhood that left her little choice but to come home after school. She created a refuge and a place of both stability and security where place is not simply material but the imaginings of a young girl. Asked if she ever read to her mother, Jada quickly responded, "Mm-hm. Oh yes, a lot. I read to her any kind of books. Like if me and my mom if it's quiet in the house, me and my mom will just sit down. She'll grab her book, I'll grab my book and we'll just read together."

Again, these moments of closeness convey adults' efforts to support children, and it is significant that Paige and Jada held onto the memory of these moments. To quote Comer (2004), children's interactions provide children with "help and approval" and convey to children "I am somebody of worth, value, and competence. 'I am. I can. I will.' These conditions . . . are the foundation of motivation" (p. 56). However, the roles that parents, grandparents, cousins, and aunts play in children's education are not always visible to teachers. Yet these brief excerpts convey an ethic of care that belies the dominant narratives, which suggest that African American families are not invested in their children's education. The stories children tell can help us as educators and researchers to reflect on our own assumptions about what African American parents value in supporting their children's education. (I use the terms *African American* and *Black* interchangeably, in keeping with scholarship on race [e.g., Greene & Abt-Perkins, 2003]).

Children's stories are part of what my colleagues and I have described elsewhere as the Adult-Child Imaginary (Greene, Burke, & McKenna, 2013). This construct acknowledges how children's experiences are shaped differently by social forces, time, and space than adults' are. In this context, the Adult-Child Imaginary distinguishes between privileged discourses used by educators and researchers to describe parent involvement and the ways in which children perceive the relationships that they have with their families across time and the many spaces where they learn, play, and develop. The Adult-Child Imaginary reminds adults involved with children to heed youth perspectives and visions because of the clarity they possess about children's contextualized needs and experiences.

Ultimately, we can learn how children perceive their families' involvement and what they believe their parents emphasize and want them to do in school (Barge & Loges, 2003; Paulson, Marchant, & Rothilsberg, 1998). Families' involvement reflects the value they place on education, the goals they have for their children, and their aspirations (Deslandes & Cloutier, 2002; Murray, 2009). However, it is important to understand the ways in which children interpret this involvement, including their perception of their parents' willingness and ability to listen to their accomplishments, monitor their daily progress in school, visit their classes, foster their talents and interests, and make known their expectations for success. At the same time, I argue that it is equally important to recognize the ways in which families "educate" their children more broadly. The examples of Paige and Jada demonstrate the extent to which families not only support literacy and a play of mind that values curiosity and inquiry, but also foster in their children cultural appreciation, the importance of family, independence, resilience, positive identity, and moral/ethical values.

Parent involvement reflects parents' orientation to the world and includes all of the multiple spaces of their lived experiences, not simply participation in school-sanctioned events. Barton and her colleagues (2004) have shown that low-income families of color are deeply committed to their children and strive to reverse a cycle of economic struggle by making sure their children are well-educated, by teaching them to believe in their own capacities to achieve, and by using their own lives as models both to emulate and avoid (Greene, 2013). Bronfenbrenner (1994) calls attention to the broad sociocultural landscape in which parent-child relationships are embedded, and describes what some might call an ecology of parent involvement. This approach, which I adopt in *Race, Community, and Urban Schools,* focuses on the roles that parents construct in the context of interacting with their children, teachers, administrators, and the community.

An ecological approach brings into focus the ways in which the roles parents construct are negotiated and framed by their own histories of schooling, by policies that limit their access to adequate resources in the neighborhood where they live, and by power that determines how resources are distributed. For example, shifts in the economy during the past 30 years have helped some families flourish, but economic factors have also hollowed out the core of urban neighborhoods with the departure of factories, limited opportunities for employment, and the loss of essential goods and services. In turn, urban renewal and gentrification (Greene, Burke, & McKenna, 2013, in press; Lipman, 2011) have had the effect of spatially isolating and marginalizing low-income families of color who do not have access to material resources, such as bookstores or libraries, proximity to stable sources of employment, public transportation, and safe spaces where children can grow and develop. A changing urban landscape has also fragmented low-income communities, so that parents can no longer rely on social networks as significant sources of capital to ensure that they might have a voice in the decision-making process that affects their children in schools (Greene, 2013). Disinvestment and funding disparities map all too neatly onto the racial and ethnic realities of schools (Ladson-Billings, 2006).

How parents envision their roles informs their sense of agency and capacity to act on their beliefs. For example, parents may view themselves as solely responsible for their child's education or believe that their child's education depends on a collaborative partnership with teachers and administrators. Hoover-Dempsey and her colleagues (1995, 2005) have observed that parents' roles reflect their sense of personal or shared responsibility for their children's educational outcomes and belief that their actions can make a difference. Parents who believe they will have the ability to influence the school's decision to place their child in special education are more likely to voice their opinions regarding the school's special education policy. In addition, parents with a stronger sense of self-efficacy are more likely to be proactive about the goals they choose to pursue, as well as having persistence in working toward the accomplishment of those goals. Importantly, parents view the educational process—and their own agency—through the lens of their own experiences in school, including both possibilities and disappointments. However, like others, Hoover-Dempsey and her colleagues (2005) appear to assume a level playing field in their accounts of parent involvement and ignore the factors of race and parents' socioeconomic backgrounds when they describe the conditions that can either foster or inhibit parent-school-community partnerships. These are factors that influence the degree to which parents believe they have agency in their children's education.

The meanings attributed to parent involvement are diverse and informed by cultural practices, how parents define the purpose of education, parents' goals for their children, and the roles they have adopted. Moreover, parent involvement can be direct or indirect, depending on a range of factors that include invitations from teachers or children (e.g., Grolnick, Ryan, & Deci, 1991), as well as the knowledge and skill that parents possess. Despite educational, linguistic, and cultural differences, families and their children possess "funds of knowledge" based on their accumulation of experiences in their everyday lives (Moll, 2005).

Indeed, parents possess valuable experiences that can have a powerful impact on children's educational experiences (Graue & Hawkins, 2010) and that teachers can build on in their classrooms. Although we tend to associate parent involvement with children's academic development, Jeynes (2005) underscores what he calls "an educationally oriented ambience" (p. 262), which he argues can have a greater impact on learning than many more general forms of involvement can have. This "ambience" is the attitude or atmosphere that forms a sense of support for children (Pushor, 2010).

THE PURPOSES OF THIS BOOK

The aim of *Race, Community, and Urban Schools: Partnering with African American Families* is to enter the ongoing conversation about low-income African American families and their role in helping their children flourish. I focus on parents' self-defined roles within the context of race, urban development, and an economy that has created opportunity for some and displaced others. More specifically, I hope to bridge the often different and conflicting experiences between White teachers and the African American families whose children they teach. Reaching this goal entails understanding the lived experiences of children and families and using their funds of knowledge as resources for teaching. Thus, this book enables readers to hear families' and children's own voices, which serve as counternarratives to a dominant rhetoric of privilege and exclusion.

Authentic, meaningful partnerships require that teachers, parent coordinators, and administrators know who parents are, what they value, and their priorities in trying to create a space for themselves in an economy that has left them behind. Moreover, as Graue (1999; Graue & Hawkins, 2010) points out, role has an ethical dimension that few researchers have examined in efforts to create home-school-community partnerships. What responsibilities are connected to defined roles? Who decides what role parents should play and in whose interests? Finally, what are parents' and educators' ethical responsibilities to one another and who has the power to determine the nature of this relationship?

I have suggested elsewhere (Greene & Abt-Perkins, 2003) that literacy researchers need to begin with where we are, and literacy is at the center of what many of us do, no matter what we teach. Educators in positions of power need to engage more fully in the process of making race visible, not simply as a mark of difference but as one of power and privilege. This entails making explicit the ways that institutions of schooling and society have placed minority students in poverty at distinct disadvantages in achieving access to quality education, housing, health care, and employment. And it means being a part of the change to ensure that literacy is not only a "civil right" (Greene, 2008) in principle, but a reality.

Inspired by my research, *Race, Community, and Urban Schools* provides a nuanced view of families, their motivations for educating their children, and their challenges in creating meaningful changes in these children's lives. *Race, Community, and Urban Schools* takes readers into neighborhoods and schools—spaces drenched in history, economic self-interest, and racial policies that determine who has access to social, economic, and cultural capital. I also identify the concrete ways families can become advocates for their children through the power of agency and community building in creating places of hope.

I provide the stories of 17 parents who participated in parent involvement workshops for 2 years at Ida B. Wells Primary Center (K–4, the name of the center is a pseudonym) in collaboration with another primary school in an economically depressed city in the Midwest. The goal of the workshops was to provide a space within the school where parents could have weekly conversations with one another and with teachers, where parents could build a network of support and share stories. The workshops also provided educators with an opportunity to learn from parents about their priorities, beliefs, values, and aspirations for their children. In referring to parents, I mean all of the family members (e.g., siblings, aunts, uncles, cousins, grandparents), friends, and neighbors who contribute to children's education and development. The parents who participated in meetings were self-selecting and, therefore, were not necessarily representative of other parents at Ida B. Wells. Not every parent had access to the resources parent meetings provided. The principal reached out to these parents because she believed increased parent involvement could help improve their children's test scores. We learned from these parents that they were far more involved than the principal and teachers fully understood. Thus, they made visible the ways they supported their children even before they attended parent meetings, and prompt us to ask what other parents may be doing of which we perhaps are unaware.

This study, discussed in Chapter 2, was part of a community-based, participatory action research project designed collaboratively and in partnership with the principal of the school, community members, and academic researchers from a local university (see Appendix A; Stoecker, 2005; Strand, Marullo, Cutforth, Stoecker, & Donohue, 2003). As part of this project, I also conducted interviews with teachers and drew upon teachers' narratives in Chapter 1 to explain what I see as a disconnect between parents' and teachers' views about parent involvement. In a separate study, discussed in Chapter 3, I interviewed children, including Paige and Jada, as part of a collaborative project with the local school district's office of research and the coordinator of a parent involvement program.

Specifically, I address the following questions: What roles do parents construct for themselves in supporting their children's education? What is the logic motivating their engagement and the roles they play? What are children's perspectives on the ways their families support their education? How do history, a developing market economy, and race shape parents' access to material resources that can both limit and foster the roles they construct for themselves? How can we characterize the relationships that families and educators create within the racialized spaces of school? How can families, communities, and educators create spaces of hope where families share power in making decisions that affect their children?

To address these questions, I draw upon Critical Race Theory (CRT) to bring into focus the racial and cultural contexts that influence parent involvement, the persistence of inequality in education despite civil rights legislation, and the value of counternarratives to give voice to the ways that parents support their children and to challenge deficit perspectives of low-income parents of color. Parents' experiences provide significant sources of knowledge for identifying forces of oppression and the assets they possess rooted in community cultural wealth (Yosso, 2005). Importantly, CRT embraces a transformative view of social action and racial justice (e.g., Delgado Bernal, 2002; Ladson-Billings & Tate, 1995; Solórzano & Yosso, 2002) and informs the community-based participatory action research that has inspired my work with parents. I also use Critical Geography, or critical policy studies, as an interpretive frame through which to recover "hidden histories" in racially coded spaces and landscapes of everyday life (Apple, 2011; Feagin, 1998; Harvey, 2007; Soja, 2010). Indeed, history is a witness to the economic policies and political processes that have influenced the resegregation of urban neighborhoods and schools and exacerbated inequality by limiting families' access to material resources and social capital (Neuman & Celano, 2001). Critical Geography helps us to see that inequality didn't just happen naturally as the result of individual decisions or market forces. It was created. One result has been to marginalize the voices of low-income families of color in decisions that affect their children. However, by focusing on these processes, such a framework does more than map out the material conditions of physical attributes of a particular geographical area. As Schein (2006) has observed, "Cultural landscapes . . . are material artifacts, with traceable and documentable empirical histories and geographies that we can use to ask questions about race in American life" (p. 5).

Unfortunately, studies of low-income minority students' underachievement emphasize pathology in a "culture of poverty," the lack of parental support and stability, high rates of students dropping out, and the extent to which schools support a school-to-prison pipeline (e.g., Edelman, 2012). The statistics can indeed be alarming. However, reports can mask larger inequities in school and in economic development that create spaces of inequality and distort our perceptions of families and children, who grow up in unsafe neighborhoods amid abandoned houses and a dearth of material resources. Embedded within these spaces are stories of "community . . . resilience, and identity formation" that can make visible the challenges that youth and their families face in their day-to-day lives (Schein, 2006, p. 14). Material spaces can limit or enable youth and their families when they seek opportunities for growth, development, and economic well-being. Just as important are the ways families re-imagine those spaces in order to take ownership of their lives and envision possible futures that transcend the material and racialized contexts of abandonment and conflict that leave families of color behind.

Few researchers studying parent involvement have examined parents' roles in the context of race and a changing political economy (but see Cucchiara, 2008; Cucchiara & Horvat, 2009; Lipman 2004, 2008, 2011; Nespor, 1997). This is an unfortunate shortcoming because researchers (e.g., Epstein, 1995, 2010; Henderson & Mapp, 2002; Hoover-Dempsey, Walker, Sandler, Whetsel, Green, & Wilkins, 2005) have under-theorized the ways that low-income minority parents navigate both opportunity and risk in supporting their children in socially isolated neighborhoods or the roles they have constructed for themselves in marginalized spaces where they have little voice in policy decisions that affect their children's life chances. Such an emphasis seems warranted given the increasing disparities in wealth between middle- and low-income families, the extent to which low-income minority children have limited access to quality schools, and the increased reliance of educators on parents to help bridge the gap between home and school.

THE ROLE OF PARENT INVOLVEMENT IN EDUCATION REFORM

Much discussion and debate have surrounded the role that parents play in their children's education, particularly in the context of widening achievement gaps and ensuring that our children are prepared for a new economy to support efforts to stabilize financial markets in the United States and Europe. President Obama reiterated these concerns in a speech focusing on his proposed reforms of No Child Left Behind based on the innovations cited in "Race to the Top." These innovations are designed to improve teacher quality with increased accountability and student achievement and a "common core" of standards. Inasmuch as the president recognized in that speech that schools need resources, including the latest textbooks, excellent teachers, and the "right" technology, he also explained that "money alone [cannot] solve our education problems." Instead, the president spoke directly to parents and urged them to take on the responsibility of supporting their children's education by "instilling a love of learning, a sense of love of learning in our kids" (Obama, 2011).

The recent recession indeed caused reductions in government spending. However, the continued shift to a market economy from a welfare state has diminished the expectation that the federal government will address structural problems that exacerbate inequality in schools and in the workplace, where low-income families struggle to earn a living wage. Indeed, those schools that are under the greatest surveillance and threat of closure are disproportionately located in low-income minority neighborhoods. As Ladson-Billings (2003) has observed, "We are experiencing an unprecedented retreat from public spaces. We relegate the 'public' to the poor and disenfranchised. Who travels on public transportation? Who lives in public housing? Who uses public health services? And, increasingly (at least in urban areas), who attends public schools?" (p. xii). Unfortunately, the erosion of public services and public spaces has placed the burden of survival on the individual households that are least able to afford to make up the difference for the withdrawal of local, state, and federal support.

The president's mandate that parents support their children's education is not new. Policy-makers have long recognized the importance of parent involvement, most notably in the Coleman Report, Title I of the Elementary and Secondary Education Act, *A Nation at Risk*, and *Becoming a Nation of Readers*. Each highlights the significant role that families play, or should play, in helping their children flourish in school. Twenty years ago, a report from the U.S. Department of Education (1987) reviewing research findings on "what works" in teaching and learning suggested that effective educational methods must regard parents as "children's first and most influential teachers" (p. 5). The authors of the guide, including former Secretary of Education William Bennett, advised parents to read to their children frequently and to incorporate literacy and numerical skills into home activities. Additionally, in 2002, then Secretary of Education Rod Paige called energetic and enthusiastic involvement from all parents "the most important help of all" in achieving effectiveness for the No Child Left Behind Act (NCLB).

A number of assumptions underlie the emphasis in the policy statements and reports of the past 25 years on the role parents can and should play: Parents serve as a bridge between home and school, animate their children's interests, and, as President Obama explained, "instill a love of learning, a sense of love of learning in our kids." The assumption is that students will do well in school if parents' goals are consistent with and support teachers' aims of instruction. If students do not do well, this reasoning implies, then parents may not be doing enough to help their children or they simply don't possess the skills, knowledge, materials, or commitment to education that teachers and policy-makers expect them to have. This latter assumption is what some have described as a cultural mismatch (e.g., Heath, 1983) and has often led to deficit theories of parent involvement that underscore what parents lack. Deficit theories are often applied to low-income minority parents whose children are more often than not the subject of concern in media portrayals of the achievement gap and in policy statements such as NCLB.

The architects of NCLB envisioned increased standards, testing, and accountability as leveling the playing field for all children and providing equity in education in the face of a widening achievement gap between Black and White students. Providing a sense of urgency and commitment to fulfilling the promise of the *Brown* decision, Secretary of Education Rod Paige described this gap as the "civil rights" issue of our time (Greene, 2008). Underlying this commitment was also the assumption that a policy embracing standards applied across the board in all schools represented a commitment to a fair, objective, and meritocratic process. It seemed to follow that if children did not flourish, then parents must not be taking advantage of the opportunities available to them. Similarly, policy-makers could blame continued achievement gaps on parents' lack of knowledge and a culture of poverty (Darling-Hammond, 2010). However, in Gutiér-rez's (2008) words, "sameness" (the same standards, the same tests, the end of the injustice of social promotion) does not provide equity or social justice any more than it redresses the "education debt" (Ladson-Billings, 2006) owed to children and families of color for past injustices. Indeed, a focus on standards, accountability, and testing has ignored the vast struc-tural inequalities that have created low achievement in the first place: the unequal distribution of funds; the lack of qualified teachers in all schools; and lack of a rich curriculum in math, science, English, social studies, and access to high-status knowledge (Lipman, 2011).

Deficit theories of parent involvement ignore the voices of parents, the roles they play in supporting and advocating for their children in mean-ingful ways outside of school, and their lived experiences. Working from a CRT perspective means respecting and acknowledging the stories of those who have experienced different forms of oppression. Understanding the roles that parents construct for themselves entails listening to their sto-ries as a challenge to a dominant narrative that represents low-income parents as "deficient" or detached from their children's education (e.g., Compton-Lilly & Greene, 2010). I argue that parents' roles are limited by the challenges they face in a changing political economy that has left low-income minority families on the margins in the United States' attempts to continue its economic dominance in a global market.

Yosso's (2005) concept of "community cultural wealth" reveals the strategies that people of color use to confront institutional structures in order to maintain or improve on their own social positions and the accu-mulated assets and resources possessed by parents and children. These re-sources include aspirational, navigational, social, linguistic, familial, and resilient capital (see also Auerbach, 2001, 2007). A sense of resilience helps children galvanize themselves against the corrosive effects of racism in schools, find ways to further their own development by creating positive relationships that support their growth, and increase their opportunities for learning. The stories or *cuentos* that families convey to their children are integral to the ways they navigate the obstacles that stand in the way of their achievement and reflect "educational strengths and strategies found in communities of color" (Delgado Bernal, 2002, p. 120).

Recent efforts to privatize schools within a free market have fore-grounded the significant role that parents can play in their children's education, but a closer examination of ideas about parental choice illustrates that parents' roles are limited to that of consumers in a competitive marketplace. There is little or no discussion of the assets that parents possess or the extent to which they might serve as partners with educators in efforts to reform schools that have been labeled as "failing." For that matter, the tendency to conceive of parents as *consumers* of educational opportunities shifts the conversation away from the role that parents play as *citizens* in a democratic society. Policy and law have promised low-income families that schools can level the playing field by offering equality, access, and opportunity. Yet the *Brown* decision neither guaranteed equal outcomes nor challenged the premise of White privilege and power that reproduces inequality and denies access to the knowledge and skills needed to function effectively within a democratic society (Kinloch, 2012). Marian Wright Edelman (2012) cites a recent Civil Rights Data Collection survey to explain persistent "inequities in school funding and educational resources [that] place students of color in low-performing schools with inadequate resources and often ineffective teachers." The practices of tracking, zero-tolerance policies, grade retention, and suspensions contribute to students' lack of engagement and increased drop-out rates. More seriously, Edelman is among a chorus of voices who describe the ways in which American education is serving as a portal to the cradle-to-prison pipeline (e.g., Sokolower, 2012; Winn & Behizadeh, 2011). Unfortunately, parents' expectations for equality and opportunity and their disappointments "shape parental expectations and influence the ways relationships are negotiated between families and schools" (Lawrence-Lightfoot, 2003, p. 113). Unless all children have equal access to a quality education and outcomes, choice becomes a "political pretense for maintaining privilege" (Furstenberg, Cook, Eccles, Elder, & Sameroff, 1999, p. 227).

As a part of the urban landscape, school is but one agent of cultural and symbolic power that has served to educate, but which has also had the power to exclude. This sense of exclusion is clearly seen in the deficit theories that have characterized the mis-education, if not the de-education, of African American students for generations. It is also difficult to ignore the disproportionate number of African American students who are placed in special education classes or in low-track classes, where they have limited access to the kind of high-status knowledge that can enable them to succeed in a global economy (e.g., Delpit, 2012).

Access to quality education remains elusive in low-income minority neighborhoods. In a climate of economic restructuring in the United States that has meant opening the free market to education, Davis Guggenheim, the director of *Waiting for Superman* (Chilcot & Guggenheim,

2010), asks important questions that bring to mind the tension between individual choice and social responsibility. He asks these questions as a father who needs to decide where he will send his own child: "What happens when schools continue to fail our kids? What is our obligation to other people's children? Did we do the right thing? Did we do enough?" The answer to the first question is unsettling because we know many low-income children and youth of color enter the school-to-prison pipeline in disproportionate numbers at a great cost to families and taxpayers. This is clear enough in the film and in current research (Sokolower, 2012). Others enter an economy that provides few rewards for the unskilled in a service economy that barely pays a living wage. The personal choices that middle-class White families make by taking public money to pursue their individual choices favor the privileged few over the common good. They leave many children behind in schools with little obligation to create meaningful change.

Their choices represent the mobility of capital and labor in a new economy that has created enormous gaps between the wealthy and the poor, not just in the workplace (knowledge workers versus a service industry of part-time and itinerant employees), but in schools, where resources are not distributed equitably (i.e., excellent teachers, educational materials, technology). In the end, Guggenheim doesn't really answer the question of whether or not "we" have done enough. This is unfortunate because he does not help resolve the tension he identifies between the exercise of choice and social responsibility in a democracy or help us understand how market forces can achieve a common good in education. Alexander (2013) has observed that "It is a great misunderstanding, indeed, a fallacy, to assume that people acting individually in their own self-interest can achieve the public good."

If parents are "choosing" to send their children to better schools outside of their neighborhoods and some distance from where their parent(s) work, those same parents become potentially disconnected from the school community. Unfortunately, Guggenheim and others fail to address how educators could work to bridge the gap between home and school in order to create the integral sense of community and belonging that is so essential to parent involvement and student achievement. Social relationships are at the core of a vital school community where families and teachers support one another with important information about academic programs and ways to prepare children to gain access to those programs.

Of concern in media portrayals of education and policy is that debate and discussion about education reform and the distribution of resources "have become shrouded in private interests" that mute parents' voices and marginalize parents' decision-making power. These private interests are what Fine (1993) referred to nearly 20 years ago as a "privatized public sphere" in which "powerful corporate interests determine educational policy" (p. 708). Meanwhile, the chasm between Black and White academic performance appears as early as kindergarten (Paige & Witty, 2010) and only widens as students advance through grade levels. By the end of 4th grade, minority students perform, on average, 2 years behind their White peers in reading and math (Cooper, 2008). By 8th grade, they have slipped 3 years behind, and by 12th grade, 4 years behind.

As long as these conditions exist, it's hard to see how schools alone can represent strength, hope, and security for many families. The academic underachievement of minority students holds dire and far-reaching social consequences. According to the 2010 *Schott 50 State Report on Public Education and Black Males* (Schott Foundation for Public Education, 2010), only 47% of Black males nationwide graduate from high school, compared to 78% of White males (a gap of 31%). In New York, the lowest-performing state in the country, the graduation rate for Black males is a mere 25%. Once out of school, former students' "idle" time increases and a corresponding plunge in lifetime wage-earning potential occurs. Unfortunately, evidence shows the increased likelihood that Black males will turn to crime in order to survive in what has become the "school-to-prison pipeline" (Children's Defense Fund, 2011). One in three Black males will be incarcerated in state or federal prison at some point during their lives, compared to only 1 in 17 White males (Sabol, West, & Cooper, 2010).

Parent involvement alone is not sufficient for educational success, but access to social, cultural, economic, and "polity capital" can enable families to gain advantage for their children. Rather than focus on any one strategy, Weiss and her colleagues (2009) emphasize "constellations of multiple localized family, institutional, and community behaviors and practices together to contribute to learning" and achieve the aim of educational equity (p. 5). Indeed, as others (Neuman & Celano, 2001) have also argued, parents need access to resources, and the lack of opportunities for low-income families exacerbates inequality. For Weiss and her colleagues, polity capital provides a way to think about the ways shared responsibility, partnerships, and collaboration can help educators and policy-makers reframe the concept of parent involvement. Polity capital shifts the focus away from individual responsibility to institutions' expectations, outreach, partnerships, and interactions with families on behalf of the child's learning and development. Such a perspective calls upon all stakeholders to work together to help children flourish and demand an increased public investment "to ensure equitable access to critically important learning opportunities" (Weiss, Bouffard, Bridglall, & Gordon, 2009, p. 6).

A CONCEPTUAL MAP OF PARENT ENGAGEMENT

To bridge the often different and conflicting experiences between teachers and families whose children they teach, I develop a framework to emphasize the complex relationships that parents have to school and the community. My framework may be a more useful analytical tool than traditional distinctions between home and school for identifying the nature of parents' involvement. To measure parents' support and efforts to advocate for the children against traditional models of parent involvement can limit our vision of what parents accomplish outside the institution of school. After all, the strategies that low-income minority parents use to guide their children may not be visible to teachers or even seen as legitimate given the emphasis that schools place on standards, accountability, and testing. Parents want their children to lead meaningful lives and flourish in a diverse society where having a good life can manifest itself in many different ways (Grant, 2012). Thus parents teach their children a sense of resilience in the face of adversity; independence; the importance of faith, family ties, civic engagement, cultural appreciation and history; and the value of maintaining high aspirations (Auerbach, 2007; Greene, 2013). As we begin to hear parents' voices and learn what they value, we can also begin to appreciate parents' lack of trust and commitment to schools. Schools have failed to educate students of color through deficit models of teaching and learning that treat difference as a deficit and have been complicit in reproducing inequality.

At the micro level, I focus on the roles that parents construct in the context of interacting with their children, teachers, and administrators. At the macro level, I also look at the ways in which the roles that parents construct are negotiated and framed by their own histories of schooling, by policies that limit their access to adequate resources in the neighborhood where they live, and by power that determines how resources are distributed. Combining a micro- and macro-level approach to parents' roles reflects the ecological approach used by Miller (2011) in mapping opportunity zones to understand both school and non-school factors on children's development and by Barton and her colleagues (2004) to explain parent engagement as a dynamic, interactive process across the multiple spaces where children's learning occurs.

Adopting an ecological perspective, I also shift away from an instrumental view of parent involvement. The parents whose voices fill these pages are deeply committed to their children. They strive to reverse a cycle of economic struggle by making sure their children are well-educated through teaching them to believe in their own capacities to achieve and using their own lives as models both to emulate and avoid. Parents' definitions of success reflect their own conceptions of what it means to have a flourishing life and can include academic competence, personal contentment and well-being, interpersonal skills, social involvement, and being safe. Moreover, parents advocate for their children and actively support them in ways that go well beyond academic issues to ensure children's health (e.g., Rogers & O'Brien, 2010). Ultimately, personal, social, and material resources inform their actions, as well as the contexts of opportunity and risk that circumscribe their lives (Furstenberg et al., 1999).

Like most American cities since World War II, the city where I met with parents experienced suburban sprawl and a shift from an industrial to a post-industrial economy. The loss of a major carmaker in 1963 was devastating. Over 7,000 people were out of work in a city of just over 100,000 as the result of the plant's closing. Since that time the city has experienced growth of just over 8% in housing, increased unemployment, and a loss of goods and services in high-poverty neighborhoods. Almost 28% of residents live below the poverty line, although a 2005 city plan (St. Joseph County Housing Consortium, 2005) reiterated an ongoing effort to market the city to high-tech corporations across the country and attract scholars to the university against a backdrop of increased poverty and segregation and a depressed housing market. The result, however, is that the "aesthetic appeal of gentrification" has given way to developers who provide abstract and decontextualized descriptions of urban spaces that rarely match the day-to-day experiences of the people who occupy those spaces. Instead, developers proffer what Haymes has described a "landscape of consumption" (Haymes, 1995, p. 97), where people with relative wealth can purchase goods, dine at upscale restaurants, and purchase a lifestyle that is urban but that also lacks the ethnic, racial, and socioeconomic diversity often associated with urban areas. Unfortunately, the needs of low-income families and working-class residents become subservient to developers' claims to the city. As a result, longtime residents, especially in rental properties, are displaced and social networks eliminated. The result may be to remove poverty from the urban core by removing minority, low-wage earners, but little is done to distribute resources more equitably

A survey done in May 2005 by the Division of Community Development and Civic Alliance identified 621 vacant and abandoned buildings in the city. These vacant and abandoned buildings are concentrated in certain neighborhoods, particularly the city's northwest side, where a 2010 study showed that 34% of the houses are identified as "unoccupied." Many of the vacant and abandoned buildings are in foreclosure after the owners defaulted on their mortgages. Police identify all of these streets as crime-ridden.

Families without stable employment are exposed to the risks that come with not having health care, insurance, childcare, or social benefits (Darling-Hammond, 2010; Furstenberg et al., 1999; Katz, 2001). Moreover, children and their families do not have easy access to community resources such as libraries, well-equipped and well-lit parks, and indoor facilities that offer opportunities for athletics, fine arts, and other programs where community bonds can be formed. As a result, children in these neighborhoods live in isolation and feel unsupported and disconnected (Greene, Burke, & McKenna, in press). Resegregation of schools (Warlick, 2011) and disinvestment in high-poverty neighborhoods have created spatialized inequality in a city that makes it difficult for low-income families of color to gain advantage for their children.

One parent recalled the changes in the city's political economy as "the beginning of the end. We lost our voices when this [auto] plant closed down. We lost our jobs, our salaries, and our power. We lost our voices." This parent's observation brings into focus the generational effects of a changing political economy, her sense that social status grants people the right to speak and to be listened to, and the extent to which they count (cf. Bourdieu, 1993). Linking voice and social status, this parent echoes Shipler's (2005) perceptions that the poor become silent and invisible in an economy that treats workers, especially Black and Latina/o families, as expendable. Shipler makes this observation poignantly when he explains that few people understand the corrosive effects of "worthlessness that course beneath the surface" (p. 126). Noreen Connell, the director of the nonprofit Educational Priorities Panel in New York, offers this observation about silence and invisibility: "If you close your eyes to the changing composition of the schools and look only at budget actions and political events . . . you're missing the assumptions that are underlying these decisions [cutbacks in education]." When minority parents try to advocate for their children, "the assumption is that these are parents who can be discounted. These are kids who just don't count—children we don't value" (cited in Kozol, 2005, p. 9).

The lack of economic, political, and social support may place children at risk, but these factors do not necessarily diminish parents' support for their children. Indeed, it is important to recognize that demographic circumstances are not absolute predictors of individual success or failure; there are other factors that can sustain and nurture success. Parents' knowledge of their children's needs can help us see that these needs are met and that the reality of their lives is reflected in our schools and classrooms. Indeed, Rodríguez-Brown (2009) points out that parents know their children's "cultural ways of learning, their knowledge, and their aspirations for their children" (p. 3).

A WHITE TEACHER-RESEARCHER AND AFRICAN AMERICAN FAMILIES

Many of the families whose lives I document in *Race, Community, and Urban Schools* moved to the city where I teach and do research in search of a safe place where they could raise their children, find employment, and ensure that their children could receive a quality education. Others have moved from one part of the city to another, motivated by a desire to "break the cycle" of poverty and limited education only to find that the struggle they faced in larger cities was ever-present in the neighborhoods where they now live. Some of the same conditions are simply inescapable in an economically depressed city. Many of these parents were unemployed when I first met them over 7 years ago, but have found ways to both turn things around economically and become strong advocates for their children and other parents. Others are still struggling to find work and remain embittered, feeling betrayed by the schools they trusted.

In one case, I watched the principal at Ida B. Wells give family members their children's scores on standardized tests at the end of a series of ten weekly workshops on parent involvement (see Chapter 2). The parents were aghast. How could their children be on the honor roll in several instances and be at the bottom 20% of the state assessment? "Why didn't the teachers tell me that my son was having trouble?" one enraged parent asked. His question was met with silence from the principal. The tension in the room was palpable. For the parent who asked this question, the meeting was a turning point. He became more involved in his sons' education, now believing that he could no longer trust teachers to educate his children. He became a member of the school's advisory board and then took a job as a teacher's aide. This is one story of personal transformation and agency that continues to evolve.

Still, there are many more families who are puzzled about how to negotiate with schools that fail to fulfill their responsibilities to students with special needs or to provide parents with access to the information they require in order to make informed decisions. I have witnessed hearings and served as an advocate for children and their families. Yet, like other educators in higher education (Purcell-Gates, 1995; Rogers, 2003), I find that I can be silenced by the experts who rationalize placing students in special education classes or on suspension.

At times, I have found it disturbing when I listened to an administrator's unwillingness to find avenues to help children succeed or who immediately blame families for their children's actions. In one particular instance, the principal of a primary school, a parent, a social worker, and I met to develop a course of action for a 9-year-old whom the principal had suspended twice. This girl had been asked to leave a Montessori school in the 1st grade; her emotional problems then followed her to public school. The principal turned to this 9-year-old and told her that she would have to take responsibility for her actions, that she would need to control her behavior. To my mind, the responsibility now rested with the principal to offer ways to get access to the kinds of long-term support that might help this little girl flourish. Children like this child fall farther and farther behind because they miss classes. I am reminded of Lawrence-Lightfoot's (2003) story of a parent, Fania, and her son, Antoine, who struggled in school:

> "Here is a kid who is bright and skilled, but totally lost and angry," she says with fury in her voice . . . . She [Fania] has tried to reach out to Antoine's teachers "humbly and without all of her emotions hanging out there. . . " "Sometimes they look at me like 'Just do it. He's got a problem, and it's his problem, not ours.'" (p. 147)

Lightfoot explains that Fania worked "not to show her rage," particularly given her sense that teachers tended to spend more time with "achieving students" and not on students like her son. "Teachers and parents need to be on the same side, especially with kids who are experiencing trouble," Fania says (p. 157). It's no longer surprising to me that the families I have witnessed with children who struggle in school are disproportionately African American in a city where public schools and neighborhoods are increasingly more racially segregated.

I was very much a part of the research that I conducted and have an unambiguous investment in seeing the families and children whose lives I chronicle throughout *Race, Community, and Urban Schools* flourish. I have spent a great deal of time with them inside and outside of school and have a perspective on their lives that teachers and administrators do not, particularly because I have seen parents interact with their children in different contexts. We shared meals together and attended films, art exhibits, and theater performances. We also talked informally on many occasions at local parks, the library, and at school, so that we developed relationships built on trust and mutual respect. As a result, parents began to see me as an advocate who could bridge the gap between school and the multiple social worlds they occupied. Still, I recognize that I am a White male researcher and a professor with all of the power and privilege that my status carries with it. I can't erase the power differential; the differences in race, gender, and class; or the access I have to resources. Given my role as researcher, it is possible that I may have inadvertently influenced some parents' views. Moreover, despite the best of intentions, I recognize that I can slip into objectifying parents or children in ways that implicate the unequal power relations between researcher and researched. With Peshkin (2000), I would argue that although researchers can never really eradicate these unequal relations of power, researchers can and should "be forthcoming and honest about how we work as researchers" (p. 9).

ORGANIZATION OF THIS BOOK

In Chapter 1, "African American Families' Engagement in School, Race, and Changes in the Political Economy," I describe a dominant narrative of parent involvement and the disconnect that often exists between parents and teachers in the ways that each group conceives of parent involvement. In turn, I challenge traditional conceptions of parent involvement and offer a conceptual framework of parent involvement that draws upon both Critical Race Theory and Critical Geography to understand the racial landscape in which parents construct roles to support and advocate for their children.

Chapter 2, "The Power of Agency and Community at Ida B. Wells Primary School," offers concrete descriptions of the roles that parents play to support and advocate for their children by monitoring and helping with homework; responding to their children's needs by teaching them self-confidence, self-reliance, and resilience; instilling in them a sense of faith and belonging; using their own lives as models of how children need to take responsibility for their own decisions; protecting them in an inhospitable environment; and finding the best programs and schools to help their children flourish. The chapter also explores how participating in parent involvement workshops helped create a network of support among parents that enabled them to start talking with teachers about their children's needs and speaking in public about the ways that other parents can advocate for their children. However, I also discuss the limits to their developing sense of agency and growth.

Chapter 3, "'We're Spending Time Together': What We Can Learn from Children About Parent Involvement," focuses on children's experiences at home, at school, and in their neighborhoods. Specifically, I tell the stories of four children who over a period of 3 years provide a window into their education and into some of the salient ways that their parents' involvement affects them. Children's stories echo parents' narratives in Chapter 2 about the ways parents help them with homework, encourage children to read, talk to children about their future, and reaffirm the values of family and community. Children offer a textured understanding of how they rely on siblings, grandparents, and other adults in developing a social network to support them academically and emotionally. We see evidence of parent involvement in the ways in which parents talk to their children and in the opportunities they provide for their children, but parents' levels of involvement can shift over time depending on their children's needs. In the end, the children whose stories I tell share a love of learning and have many assets that teachers can build on in fostering literacy, but children's stories also teach us something about the adverse effects that increased testing and accountability have had on children and families.

Chapter 4, "Schools as Inclusive and Exclusionary Spaces," focuses on schools as ideological spaces that have excluded people of color. I draw upon parents' life histories to tell a story of their experiences in school. Many parents' teachers did not seem interested in their well-being as students or as young people who struggled in difficult economic circumstances. Now, as adults, they are neither invited to participate in key decisions that affect their children's future nor are they privy to policies about curriculum, increased testing, standards, or accountability. However, despite their positive and negative experiences in schools, parents convey a sense of urgency in supporting their children motivated by a profound faith that education can reverse a cycle of under-education and poverty. Listening to parents means grasping the complexity of silence and learning to shift a rhetoric of blame to structural explanations that describe schools as exclusionary spaces that marginalize parents of color.

Chapter 5, "Families as Advocates in Creating Spaces of Hope at Home, in Schools, and in the Community," offers a framework of parent involvement that envisions parents as advocates and decision-makers who can make a difference in their children's lives. I argue that parents need opportunities for democratic engagements that enable them to identify and critique structural problems that limit the equal distribution of resources in schools and their communities. Schools can collaborate with parents in forging relationships with community partners to create a wide network of support to help them flourish. Such a network can provide political leverage to affect a more equitable distribution of resources and level the playing field through what Sampson, Morenoff, and Gannon-Rowley (2002) have described as "collective efficacy."

Listening to parents' voices helps us see the extent to which what matters most to families is often not visible to educators, and that parent involvement need not be construed solely as parents' efforts to support their children's performance on standardized test scores. Thus, it is important that educators understand more fully who parents are, and what they are already doing to support their children, and develop a framework of parent involvement that is both reciprocal and collaborative.

CHAPTER 1

African American Families' Engagement in School, Race, and Changes in the Political Economy

I listened to Keisha, who explained that she lives "her dreams through her children. I kinda give 'em my story and that helps them kinda make 'em go a little bit further, kinda give 'em inspiration." I listened to Amy, who supported the children in her neighborhood and created a sense of community with other single mothers. Together they sat at a dining room table where they passed around a chapter book and gave each child an opportunity to read a page. At times, a child struggled with a word and Amy mentioned that she had to help some of the children sound out words they didn't recognize. Importantly, Amy and the other mothers were careful to let the children figure out the words—to be patient with the children. And the mothers modeled the value of reading aloud when it was their turn. I listened to Beatrice, who reflected on the challenges that she faced in helping her sons flourish in school: "Yeah, the boys are different. They're harder to get focused on doing homework and just sitting still pretty much. The girls, they just come in, and the boys know the routine, they just refuse to do the routine." Beatrice acknowledged these differences with a sense of compassion and understanding.

Educators have pointed out that children can be more resistant to the culture of school where teachers reward and encourage disciplined, quiet, individual behaviors (Ferguson, 2001). Unfortunately, the cultural practices of school can work against children's (both boys and girls) more social, collaborative, and even competitive instincts. Thus it is not surprising that children disengage. However, Beatrice would not let this happen. She conveyed her commitment to all of her children's education and spoke of the ways that she orchestrated opportunities for learning. She created a space for them at home where they could do their schoolwork and where she expected them to help one another.

Keisha, Amy, and Beatrice told stories of "lovingly" and "patiently" teaching their children to read. They used a lifetime of learning, economic hardship, and missed opportunities as teachable moments and they found innovative ways to reach out to their children even if their children resisted school. When I reflect upon these stories, I am puzzled by the research I read that characterizes low-income parents as "detached," "disengaged," or "uninvested" in their children's education (Compton-Lilly, 2003; Dudley-Marling, 2009). Commonsense explanations of why children fail often assign responsibility to children's families and fuel dominant narratives that focus on deficits without fully understanding the roles parents play in their children's lives. I have tried in my research to square the stories of parents' involvement and research to understand the source of deficit theories and to make visible the strategic, intentional ways that parents are involved. The disconnect between parents' and teachers' perceptions of what it means to be involved results from the different roles parents and teachers assign one another in supporting children's education, the lack of opportunities to speak with one another directly, and the limited time they have to listen to one another's concerns (e.g., Greene & Long, 2010). However, researchers (e.g., Noguera, 2001) also attribute this disconnect to differences in racial, ethnic, and socioeconomic backgrounds between parents and educators. Parents have different needs, beliefs, and opinions that shape how they view their role in school and the purposes of education.

I learned from teachers at Ida B. Wells that they were well-meaning in their efforts to motivate parents to sign up to help in classrooms, accompany children on field trips, and attend events in the evening, including an open house at the beginning of the year, concerts, reading night, movie night, and game night. Teachers wanted parents to be more of a presence in school as a sign of parents' engagement. They also wanted parents to "reinforce what they were doing in class," as one teacher explained, by making sure that their children completed their homework and practiced the skills teachers taught in class. (See Appendix B for a discussion of the methodology for interviewing teachers.) However, teachers I have spoken with were often unaware of parents' efforts to support their children and were less than certain that parents possessed the knowledge they needed to help their children. For example, one 4th-grade teacher explained:

> I'm not so sure parents really know what they're supposed to do with the academics, and I don't think my parents can read, or I don't think my parents can write. I think my parents don't know how to bring their child along. I don't think they know how they are supposed to study these sight words. How are we supposed to study these word families? How are we supposed to study? How do we work on comprehension? How do I sit down and read with my child

in an effective way? I think that's the thing that a lot of our parents don't get.

With few opportunities to learn what parents know or didn't know, the teacher was left to theorize on her own about the reasons why the children she taught struggled in her classroom. She assumed that parents were not really equipped to help their children, that parents did not have the capacity to teach their children comprehension strategies, sight words, and word families. Reading researchers have offered an alternative explanation for children's struggles with reading. Success in reading depends on the children's level of engagement, their interests, and the extent to which the children's reading materials are culturally relevant. Indeed, Compton-Lilly (2007) observes that "Learning is contingent on a range of factors—from providing experiences that are appropriate for particular children to engaging those children in thoughtful, active, stimulating, and critical learning experiences" (p. 34). My concern in conveying the story of this one particular teacher is that she uses language that treats parents as "other" and attributes children's difficulties to a deficit perspective of parent involvement.

Another teacher tried to understand the extent to which parents and educators may not fully understand one another's perspective about the ways they can help children flourish. She used the metaphor of a "barrier," or "block," to explain what I also see as the spatial distance that often exists between educators and parents. Implicitly, she challenges us to understand how to bridge the gap between the world that separates parents and educators by race, class, gender, and ethnicity and how to "come together to reach that goal." In addition, she prompts educators to think about ways to reach out to parents. Still, she attributes some of the problems that she faces as an educator to parents' lack of capacity:

> There's this block as far as, I think in general, across the United States, that the parents are on one side and the teacher and the school is on the other side. But everybody really wants the same thing. It's just how to come together to reach that goal. . . . And, I think neither side really knows how to come about that, and I see it being more of an outreach from the school side than the parents' side, because the parents are in a different place. They don't have as much capability to plan things out. And I think when some parents want to get involved, it's not so readily acceptable.

Providing a broad sense of the problem, she struggles to find ways to develop a common vision without really grounding her observations in the day-to-day lives of the children and families at Ida B. Wells. In the end, I wonder how she came to the conclusion that parents do not have the "capability to plan things out" or that parent involvement is "not readily acceptable."

The metaphors that teachers at Ida B. Wells employed to describe the difficulties of partnering with parents seemed to go hand-in-hand with the social categories they used to name parents' experiences. Underlying their efforts to reach out to parents were subtle references teachers made to cycles of poverty across generations in families, the growing number of single-parent households at Ida B. Wells, and the realities of teaching in an "urban," "inner-city," public school. I listened to teachers easily slip from observations about urban decay in the inner city to moral imperatives that cast families in a negative light. "These are children raised by children," one teacher remarked, while another described the extent to which she believed that parents simply "burn the candle at both ends" to explain why parents are not more involved.

Still another teacher described the context of Ida B. Wells and then offered a generalized account of parents' limited skills in raising their children, the lack of models in parents' own upbringing, the challenges they face in trying to juggle parenting and work responsibilities, and even the neglect created by addiction:

> Well, just working in an inner-city school, I realize that there are a lot of parents who don't have great parenting skills either because they didn't see any when they were growing up or they're working excessive hours or there are addiction issues or whatever.

This kind of overgeneralized account of "urban" families living in poverty fuels stereotypes, and ultimately affects teachers' expectations of their students.

One teacher offered a bit of a corrective to deficit perspectives of parents and explained that she needed to be flexible, show parents that she cared, and recognize the broader context of parents' and children's day-to-day lives. Another teacher echoed this teacher's focus on context and took aim at structural issues and the lack of resources in children's homes and at school:

> Most of the problems that we face are not just in education but in our world, in our society, have to do with poverty, want, neglect, those kinds of things. People who don't have enough time, people who don't have enough resources, and are in a position of having to parent.

For that matter, this teacher also pointed out that schools themselves don't have enough resources and that teachers need to understand what parents are doing for their children in an economy that has placed an enormous burden on low-income families.

Embedded within teachers' explanations of parent involvement is a set of binaries between home and school, experience and expertise, everyday learning and achievement in school, and parent and teacher. These binaries are ideological, historical, and structural. They are informed by race, class, and power. Thus I would argue that teachers' metaphors are not neutral, objective ways of explaining parent involvement. In fact, studies underscore the extent to which institutions like school embed stories of race, power, and injustice (e.g., Compton-Lilly, 2007; Lewis, 2003). The racialized language of deficit is very much in line with a prevailing rhetoric in research (Epstein, 2010), the media (Kohn, 2013), and op-ed pages (Brooks, 2013). The stories we tell one another have become part of a dominant narrative that attributes children's failures to their parents and families.

The rhetorical designations that are so much of a part of the dominant discourse in education also represent the interpretive frameworks that many teachers use to categorize families as part of an "invisible code" (Graue & Hawkins, 2010). Watson (2011) also explains that teachers' perceptions of "urban" are equivalent to race, "specifically Black and Latina/o—and often *poor*." More striking are the assumptions that are embedded in notions of urban and poor. As one teacher in Watson's study put it: "To me, urban students come from an environment where they can't see the value of education. They can't see why it matters, because everyone that they know, everything that they do, has nothing to do with having an education." Brooks (2013) offers this more recent iteration of the problem of promulgating unsupported and unattributed claims about low-income families whom he feels would benefit from universal preschool: "Millions of parents don't have the means, the skill or, in some cases, the interest in building their children's future." Such a conclusion circulates in the popular media and tends to be repeated without much critical debate, and dehumanizes families.

Lawrence-Lightfoot (2003) has helped me understand something of the challenges we face as educators if we are committed to creating meaningful partnerships with parents informed by principles of democratic participation and social justice. In one poignant example, she recalled the dissonant relationship that existed between her parents and her teachers, which was replicated with her own daughter's teacher. Haunted by the past, Lawrence-Lightfoot "was drawn back in time, immediately made to feel small, powerless, and infantilized" when she went to meet her daughter's teacher for a parent-teacher conference (p. xviii). Nothing in her academic experience could prepare her for the "terror" of meeting with her daughter's teachers or the "subtle institutional barriers that made her [feel] strangely unwelcome . . . as if she were trespassing on foreign ground." Lawrence-Lightfoot goes on to explain how these "tiny scenes played out the larger social and cultural issues [race, class, and gender] in our society" (p. xviii). To listen to parents would invite them to explain the ways in which they are involved, to define parents' and teachers' roles and responsibilities to one another, and to participate in a more democratic decision-making process about the kinds of schools that are meaningful to parents and children. A more democratic process would also prompt educators to recognize the power dynamic that has excluded and silenced parents.

ASSUMPTIONS ABOUT PARENT INVOLVEMENT

Traditionally, the story of parent involvement starts with Lyndon B. Johnson's War on Poverty and the subsequent Coleman (1966) Report, which called attention to a combination of factors that influence students' educational achievement, including school composition (i.e., who attends a given school), teaching, environment, and family background. The government implemented Head Start and a number of interventions to mitigate the effects of poverty on children and families of color and redress the consequences of legal segregation in a system that rarely ensured that separate was ever equal. A number of studies (for a review, see Henderson & Mapp, 2002) emerged during the next 20 years to test a number of key assumptions: that parent involvement contributes significantly to children's achievement; that factors in families matter in charting students' academic progress, including socioeconomic background, parents' level of education, and race; the extent to which families form partnerships with schools; and finally, that parents' involvement in the community can make a difference for their children's learning and achievement.

The era following the publication of the Coleman Report was indeed a "vibrant" period of research and serves as an important touchstone for studies of parent involvement. Many of these studies (for a review, see Rodríguez-Brown, 2009) were designed to evaluate the effects of programs and other interventions. Others looked at the ways in which families are involved with their children's learning, with particular attention to the relationship between family background (family income, education, occupation, ethnicity, and culture) and student achievement; at the differences between how families of lower- and higher-performing children are engaged in their learning; and at the ways in which parents are involved at home (monitoring homework and time use, talking about school, and planning for the future) and at school (attending events, meeting with teachers, and volunteering) and their effects on student performance (Lee & Bowen, 2006). As Ladson-Billings (2006) points out, however, the tendency has been to overemphasize the relationship between family background and educational attainment. As a consequence, family background has become the focus of school and policy decisions.

Moreover, many of these studies and subsequent models failed to recognize how families conceive of parent involvement, the assets that families possess, or the extent to which home-school relationships existed on an uneven playing field. For example, Epstein's (2010) model, developed at the same time that reports on education in the 1980s began to signal a crisis in education (e.g., *A Nation at Risk* and *What Works*), set the context for her work and others—to establish ways that parents can support schools. With increased immigration and a changing demographic in urban schools, policy-makers grew anxious about the erosion of cultural literacy and the loss of a shared sense of beliefs and values between educators and families.

The assumption in government reports such as *What Works* was that educators could give low-income African American and Latina/o families the information they needed to support children's home literacy and literacy readiness. Involving families would support teachers who were uncertain about how to reach children and youth as the gaps between African American and White and wealthy and poor continued to widen. Parent involvement was and continues to be an ideological issue, as much if not more so than a disciplinary one in current reform efforts that are still based on standards, accountability, testing, and "disciplining" low-performing schools in low-income minority neighborhoods.

Ironically, even as reports such as *A Nation at Risk* (National Commission on Excellence in Education, 1983) described education as the linchpin of economic competitiveness, the report ignored the context of enormous economic crisis and change in a post-industrial age. During this period, Americans witnessed the outsourcing of manufacturing overseas and a society that created disparities between high-income professionals and low-wage earners in a service economy that offered families little security in the form of pensions and health insurance (Lipman, 2011). This economic restructuring disproportionately affected African American families whose children struggled in low-income, under-resourced, hyper-segregated schools. More importantly, as Darling-Hammond (2010) has asserted, the call for reform was more rhetorical than real; most targeted federal programs supporting investments in college access and

K–12 schools in urban and poor rural areas were reduced or eliminated during the Reagan administration in the 1980s, as were social and economic programs that had the potential to change the life paths for many low-income families.

Recent studies have indeed established the value of parent involvement and offered insights into the differences in family structure between low- and middle-class parents (Lareau, 2003); the factors that explain why parents are involved, such as the roles parents construct for themselves as supporters and advocates for the children (Auerbach, 2007); and the extent to which the construction of these roles depends on parents' sense of efficacy to be involved in ways that make a difference (Hoover-Dempsey, Walker, Sandler, Whetsel, Green, & Wilkins, 2005). In addition, studies have also helped explain the leadership roles (Auerbach, 2011) that teachers and administrators play in helping to forge relationships with parents and helping them feel a sense of belonging in school.

Importantly, a number of ethnographic studies have shown the extent to which African American families support literacy at home and in their neighborhoods as part of their everyday lives. They have also shown that the children of these families are quite successful in school (Compton-Lilly, 2003, 2007; Taylor & Dorsey-Gaines, 1988; Teale, 1986). Ethnographic studies should prompt all of us to reconsider our assumptions about African American children and their families and the idea that children come to school with a dearth of literacy experiences. I would argue that parents' involvement has remained constant for generations (e.g., Perry, Steele, & Hilliard, 2003), but parents' efforts have gone unnoticed by educators who embrace a dominant model of parent involvement.

Unfortunately, educators have not always been trained to know how to build on the funds of knowledge that students bring from their home and community cultures or to look beyond discourses about parents of color that circulate in schools, discussions about policy, and research. The challenge for educators is to gain a deep understanding of families' histories and cultures in order to bridge home and school and understand the variations within families that are different from our own. Meaningful change entails replacing mainstream deficit theories of parent involvement with an alternative discourse that reflects the lived experiences of children and their families.

TRADITIONAL MODELS OF PARENT INVOLVEMENT

Research (for a review, see Compton-Lilly & Greene, 2010) on parenting and parent involvement stresses the extent to which parents provide the emotional and cognitive building blocks of learning through trust and open communication; the importance of cognitive stimulation at home through play (e.g., games); and the use of language, including shared book reading. A consistent theme in this research is that "children of lower socioeconomic status are exposed to less educationally rich home environments" than middle- and upper-middle-class professional families (Weiss et al., 2009, p. 20; see also reviews by Henderson & Mapp, 2002, and by Rodríguez-Brown, 2009). Hart and Risley (1995) and Lareau (2003) explain differences in the types (e.g., questioning strategies, elaboration) and quantity of talk that parents use to foster early childhood development. Studies also stress the value of academic socialization (i.e., parents convey that they value education and have high expectations) as a means for motivating children, particularly when parents help their children feel competent; the value of talking about current and future education (building this knowledge is critical to achieve equity); the importance of monitoring and rule-setting; and the value of helping with homework, particularly when it supports "autonomy, self-management, and self-regulatory skills" (Weiss et al., 2009, p. 21).

Traditional forms of parent involvement derive from White middle-class values that privilege participating at school, whether through attending meetings, accompanying children on field trips, or joining organizations such as the PTO (e.g., Li, 2010). Epstein's (e.g., 1995, 2010) model, which is based on overlapping spheres of home, school, and community influences that shape students' learning and development, remains the ground against which many educators measure parent involvement. This model also includes a six-part typology of forms of parent involvement that schools should promote: basic obligations of parenting, home-school communication, volunteering at school, learning at home, school decision-making, and community-school connections.

In developing her model of building relationships between home and school, Epstein focuses primarily on the obligations that families have to teachers, not the obligations that schools have to families or the ethical responsibility that teachers and parents might have to one another. Epstein's model also assumes a level playing field between parents and teachers. However, in making this assumption, Epstein fails to account for the ways in which power and ideology affect the interactions of what she describes as overlapping spheres of influence between home and school. Finally, her model does not address parents' sense of agency or capacity for decision-making and collaboration in a partnership aimed at supporting children's academic learning. There is no space in this model for negotiation or for schools to assume responsibilities that serve the needs of parents, what they bring to the table, or how the needs of the school affect what they need. Teachers simply define the context for parents to support their children's learning in what Graue (1999) describes as "a universalistic perspective on interactions between families and the institution of school" (p. 6) that reinscribes power and privilege by determining whose voices count and whose voices do not.

When measured by traditional forms of involvement such as volunteering in children's classrooms, research (e.g., Englund, Luckner, Whaley, & Egeland, 2004) continues to affirm a dominant narrative that depicts parents with low socioeconomic status (SES) as less involved in their children's education than higher-SES parents. Lareau (2003), in particular, portrays low-SES parents as less likely to supplement curriculum with closely related work at home, encourage their children's talents, challenge teachers' expertise, and communicate with other parents about their children's education. She draws these conclusions based on what she sees middle- and high-income parents doing to support their children.

Unfortunately, Lareau's (2003) study suggests that differences in parenting are deficiencies in the ways in which low-income parents support their children in school. However, it would be a mistake to assume that low-income parents do not support their children's education because the level and type of involvement do not mirror those of middle- and high-income parents. A more accurate reading of Lareau's conclusions is that teachers simply devalue the sense of family, resourcefulness, and independence that many lower-income children may be more likely to learn at home (e.g., Auerbach, 2007; Rodríguez-Brown, 2009). These skills stand in strong contrast to the sense of innate privilege that youth from middle- and high-income families learn, which enable them to "negotiate" institutional power. Indeed, Lareau and her colleagues (e.g., Horvat, Weininger, & Lareau, 2003) have shown that schools often give greater legitimacy to the concerns voiced by middle-class families whose cultural capital (e.g., beliefs and values) is more consistent with school administrators and teachers. Still, as Valdés (1996) points out, the way to empower parents is not to transform low-income parents into high- and middle-income parents, but to acknowledge the legitimacy of what parents value and build on these values in providing support.

AN ALTERNATIVE DISCOURSE OF PARENT INVOLVEMENT

Strengthening families and communities will facilitate increased engagement with their children's education. Doing so requires that educators and teachers listen to families' voices and recognize the complexity of the problems that they seek to address in their day-to-day lives. Such a view is essential in the ways that educators train teachers to develop partnerships with families. Families' engagement in their children's education is inextricably linked to their personal histories, the legacies of their families' education, and the ways in which policies have shaped their experiences. That is, a number of different contexts influence parents' beliefs in the utility, power, and purpose of education. In particular, we cannot let our own perceptions of school as a potential source of success limit our understanding of the multiple contexts that have marginalized African American families in their efforts to gain access to quality education and wealth. Unfortunately, Tillman (2004) points out, while "cultural, social, and economic differences may position African American parents as outsiders in school as they are presently structured, it is not necessarily the case that these parents are uninterested" (p. 169).

Parents need to know that educators are listening and value their voices/objectives in any effort to build parent-family-school partnerships. This was Fine's (1993) argument nearly 20 years ago and it remains relevant: "Parents enter the contested public sphere of public education typically with neither resources nor power. They are usually not welcomed, by schools, to the critical and social work of rethinking educational structures and practices" (p. 683). Therefore, efforts to engage parents should serve the interests of children and their families, not just schools. Moreover, whether or not parents will be partners in children's education is a function of a school's willingness and ability to recognize, respect, and address families' needs, as well as differences in race and culture.

However, crossing boundaries is probably easier when parents whose values, histories, culture, and life circumstances are more similar to the those of the teacher. But this is rarely the case in inner-city schools where the majority of students and their families are African American and Latina/o and teachers are White. As educators, we cannot ignore the fact that inner-city schools are becoming more segregated (Kozol, 2005; Orfield & Gordon, 2001) and parents do not see themselves in administrative positions or in classrooms. The story that this lack of diversity tells parents is powerful, especially when their children are not flourishing (Tatum, 2007).

What "works" for one family at one point in time within a given context will not necessarily work with other families in other contexts, especially when we consider the fact that not all families have access to the same economic and educational resources. Moreover, culture is a fluid concept that encompasses the lived experiences and practices of students and their families rooted in history, geography, language, and community (Gutiérrez & Rogoff, 2003). Individuals' beliefs, values, and worldview give meaning to their lives, but culture is neither bound by race nor ethnicity (Howard, 2010).

AFRICAN AMERICAN PARENTS' ROLES
IN A CHANGING POLITICAL ECONOMY

In this section, I consider a set of theoretical constructs that can help educators and researchers think about an ecology of parent involvement that is connected to race, power, and policies in education and economic development. The relationships that families develop are nested within communities (e.g., school, work, health activities, places of worship, recreation), history, and policies that affect a given child's future. The relationships that families forge in these different communities foreground the range of ways that families are engaged in "educating" their children, not just at school but at home and where they worship, play, and work. As I have suggested thus far, policy-makers have assumed an equal playing field in creating standards as a vehicle for equity and that children's failure in school can be attributed to parents' failure to take advantage of opportunities, to their lack of knowledge and skill, and to a "culture of poverty." This is at best a rhetoric that ignores the ways that schools reproduce inequality. Moreover, educational policies that impose uniform standards, in the context of a changing political economy, have placed low-income African American families at a disadvantage, despite the gains made in civil rights law.

As I suggested earlier, researchers tend to emphasize family background to explain student achievement. Thus, educators traditionally expect families to support their children's education by helping with homework, inspiring a love of learning, and participating in events at school. Still, a number of factors contribute to continuing gaps in achievement (Berliner, 2014; Darling-Hammond, 2010; Rothstein, 2004):

- A high level of poverty (in a service economy where even full-time employment leaves families below the poverty level unable to provide a full range of care for their children) and low levels of social support for low-income children's health and welfare
- The unequal allocation of school resources in high-poverty, racially segregated schools
- Inadequate systems for providing high-quality teachers who provide culturally relevant instruction to meet the needs of all students
- Rationing high-quality education through tracking (i.e., high-status vs. low status)

In mapping out a typography of parents' roles, I have relied on Auerbach (2007), who explains that parent roles and social position are best represented along a continuum from "less proactive to more proactive" and from "supporters to advocates" that exists within an institutional context of unequal relations of power. By theorizing parents' roles in this way, Auerbach brings into sharp relief the ways that parents' constructed roles exist in a context of "broad inequalities" (p. 251) that can silence and marginalize low-income minority parents. Moreover, Auerbach calls attention to the ways that parents adopt multiple roles that can also evolve over time as they negotiate ways to gain advantage for their children at home, at school, or in the community (see also Barton, Drake, Perez, St. Louis, & George, 2004).

To understand the role that race plays in parent involvement and the persistence of inequality in school, I also draw upon Yosso's (2005) conception of "community cultural wealth." Specifically, Yosso's (2005) conception of "community cultural wealth" reveals the strategies used by people of color to confront institutional structures to maintain or improve on their own social positions. With others (e.g., Auerbach, 2007; Delgado Bernal, 1998, 2002), Yosso argues that oppression has long engendered a sense of agency, self-reliance, resistance, and social movements that have sought to provide access and equity through education (Anderson, 1988; Fisher, 2009). To ignore a legacy of education borne of struggle is to engage in a purposeful kind of forgetting.

By focusing her research on the experiences of families and their children, Yosso reveals the depth and variety of accumulated assets and resources that families possess. Additional research is warranted so that we may understand the kinds of capital that low-income minority parents use to support their children's education and the ways they can navigate institutional authority to create change.

Critical Race Theory (CRT) offers a lens through which to learn about the rich cultural knowledge that socially marginalized groups possess in the form of counternarratives. As both a methodological and epistemological tool, counternarratives (e.g., chronicles, stories, testimonies) have the capacity to challenge seemingly neutral policies based on a meritocracy to more fully understand the racialized nature of spaces and the institutional, structural, and ideological reproduction of inequality. CRT presses the questions of whose knowledge counts and whose knowledge is discounted in studies that overgeneralize about family background and educational success.

CRT and its progenitor, Critical Legal Studies, have critiqued the rules of "law as guarantor of racial justice" in the context of the "unraveling of liberal reform" and the "retreat of politics and law from civil rights advocacy" (Crenshaw, 2011, p. 1261). As in the work of DuBois (2009), Woodson (2012), and others in such fields as ethnic studies and women's studies, history, critical geography, and sociology, theorists have sought to unmask notions of objectivity to reveal the extent to which race and racism are a permanent, enduring part of American culture that explains the depths of inequality in schooling and society (e.g., Ladson-Billings & Tate, 1995; Lopez & Parker, 2003; Matsuda, Lawrence, Delgado, & Crenshaw 1993). In turn, CRT has shown how rule of law has helped rationalize existing racial power and the ways in which law reproduces inequality. After all, no neutral concept of merit can justify the "unequal distribution of wealth, power, and prestige in America" (Crenshaw, 2011, p. 1309) that we witness in low-income urban neighborhoods and their schools.

For some researchers (Lareau, 2003; Rothstein, 2004), the lack of opportunities available for minority families may seem like class issues, not the consequences of race. However, Lewis (2003, 2008) argues that it would be a mistake to talk about one without the other, given a long history of state-sponsored segregation and policies that have limited African Americans' access to wealth. These include the federal government's underwriting of rules for Federal Housing Authority guidelines, racially restricted housing covenants, exclusionary zoning ordinances, banks' redlining practices, and racial steering by real estate agents (e.g., Massey & Denton, 1993; Santow, 2007; Squires & Kubrin, 2005).

Lewis (2003) argues further that exclusionary practices and racialized policies in housing, schooling, and employment explain gaps in wealth. In 2009, African American families in the United States had a median net worth of $20,600, which was just 14.6% of the median net worth of White families (Watkins, 2012). By 2011, the typical White family had 20 times the wealth of the median African American family (Fessler, 2011) and 18 times that of Latina/o households, according to a Pew Research Center (Kochhar, Fry & Taylor, 2011) analysis of newly available government data from 2009. These lopsided wealth ratios are the largest since the government began publishing such data a quarter of a century ago, and roughly twice the size of the ratios that had prevailed among these three groups for the 2 decades prior to the current recession. Moreover, biases in housing have cost African Americans upwards of $2 billion given the disparity in home financing markets, with an average of $20,000 for those families holding mortgages (Squires & Kubrin, 2005).

Fiscal disparities and state-sponsored racism contribute to what Ladson-Billings (2006) has described as the "education debt." She uses this phrase to challenge current discourse about the "achievement gap," which, for her, places responsibility on students and families of color to change in ways that will narrow that gap. However, focusing on individual responsibility alone ignores the structural inequalities that have placed low-income children of color at a disadvantage in schools that lack the resources that they need to flourish. It is fair to say that achievement on standardized tests says more about access to economic opportunity than anything else (Rose, 1988) in a racialized landscape where the contours of racial inequality flow directly from the past (e.g., racial ordinances, restrictive covenants, redlining, blockbusting, private deed restrictions). Educational achievement and attainment reflect directly on economic disparities that find their source in segregation, discrimination, and a political economy that funnels resources away from low-income neighborhoods (Berliner, 2014).

Parents navigate their roles in their children's education amid the racial and economic contexts that limit their decisions and roles as parents. Importantly, Lewis (2008) has pointed out that conceptions of race have remained "collectively too focused on people's individual dispositions and ignore how racial inequality is built into our structures and organizations" (p. 74; Greene & Abt-Perkins, 2003). As a social construct, race is not simply a social category or abstraction that can be used as a variable to draw correlations between family background and children's achievement. The meanings people ascribe to difference affect how people of color see themselves; where they live, work, and go to school; and the extent to which they have access to material resources.

Schools are complicit in framing ideas about race and, as racialized spaces, they position students in ways that influence the development of students' literate identities while also limiting students' life chances. According to Crenshaw (2011), schools are

> the primary means for imbuing people with values, certain political beliefs, and a specific cultural character. Furthermore, in any social system, teaching is done within definite ideological parameters that engender common frames of reference and orientation among the people. The assumptions a person conceives will in large measure . . . form one's perception of reality. (p. 1305)

Race is used as a sorting mechanism and studies consistently demonstrate the extent to which teachers place low-income minority students in low-track classes that prepare them for low-paying jobs in a service economy (Lipman, 2011; Oakes, 2005; Oakes & Guiton, 1995) that caters to a new industry of information workers. Brandt (2001) has observed that while literacy has undeniably served as an "instrument for more democratic access to learning, political participation, and upward mobility . . . it has become one of the sharpest tools for stratification and denial of opportunity" (p. 2). And perhaps most relevant to my study of parent involvement, Noguera (2001) has pointed out that perceptions of race and class affect the extent to which school administrators treat low-income

African American and Latina/o parents differently than White middle-class parents (Lareau, 2003; Lareau & Horvat, 1999).

I have argued that it is important to understand parent involvement at the intersection of education policy and a changing political economy. Shifts in the economy have begun to transform the urban landscape through developing gentrified spaces to create markets and attract wealth, while also disinvesting in low-income minority neighborhoods. As Hall and Cole-Robinson (in press) point out, urban renewal only reduces poverty by displacing minority families from the "urban core rather than equalizing the distribution of social wealth." For that matter, they argue that the practice of gentrification intensifies the polarization between displaced citizens and people of relative wealth, thereby cultivating what Berliner (2014) describes as "apartheid-lite systems of schooling." Low-income minority parents are left to navigate opportunities and risks in a context in which both education and economic policies have the potential to exacerbate inequality by limiting access to quality education and material resources that low-income minority children and families rely on to flourish.

The rhetoric of gentrification calls attention to the blight of low-income neighborhoods. In reality, gentrification seeks to refashion a cultural identity that exists within a framework of race, class, and ethnicity. This is particularly true with the construction of private homes in newly gentrified spaces, historically associated with individuality and the White middle class in suburbs after World War II, and the displacement of low-income minority families who rent apartments and homes that are often owned by absentee landlords. This sense of privacy brings with it a sense of exclusion that once manifested itself through racial covenants, real estate steering, and government lending programs. Although fences may not serve as physical markers of privacy, the wealth and privilege associated with new housing serve as markers of "class distinction," "racial identity," and White privilege (Harris, 2006, p. 148). Kevin Fox Gotham has noted that "privacy starts at the property boundary and is related to the deed of ownership and an entire ideology that is encapsulated within it, such that the discussions of private property rights must be viewed as a language of exclusion" (quoted in Harris, p. 130). Excluded are those perceived as "other," including youth, and especially youth of color, who threaten the safety of White families of relative wealth. One of the outcomes that Hall and Cole-Robinson identify is "the 'pushing out' and 'keeping out' of urban and minority occupants in order to add to the attractiveness of city living."

I use Critical Geography, or Critical Policy Studies, as a lens though which to analyze the racial and cultural contexts of urban development, especially the shifts that have occurred since a market economy has begun to replace the welfare state of the New Deal (Apple, 2006, 2011; Feagin, 1998; Harvey, 2007, 2009; Soja, 2010). Critical Geography brings a critical perspective to recent shifts in the economy by understanding the urban landscape spatially, historically, and socially. Like CRT, Critical Geography not only seeks to critique inequality, but adopts an activist stance toward creating meaningful change to mitigate the effects of poverty, urban decay, and inequality.

In cities across America's Rust Belt, such as the one where I have participated in and led parent meetings, it is common for city leaders to step in with money, develop new roads and sidewalks, sell land well below market value, and offer other incentives to encourage economic growth. In turn, developers demolish houses in "blighted areas" occupied by low-income African American and Latina/o families and replace communities with gentrified spaces designed to attract new forms of capital and a professional class that can afford expensive housing. In many instances, these gentrified spaces exist alongside low-income minority neighborhoods and accentuate fiscal disparities and power that inevitably create two cities. The features of the new American city are contradictory, inscribed in the skeletal remains of factories, mills, and steel plants, blocks of boarded-up abandoned houses, ethnic festivals, free outdoor concerts, and farmers' markets (e.g., Feagin, 1998; Lipman, 2011; Smith, 2008; Wacquant, 1995).

Redevelopment comes at a price for low-income minority families in the form of tax abatements that release private developers from paying property taxes that would normally be applied to school budgets and libraries in the inner city. Similarly, city leaders and redevelopment boards create Tax Incremental Funds (TIFs), which exacerbate inequality by redirecting taxes from education to building infrastructure for gentrified neighborhoods that are marketed to professionals in an information economy. These decisions affect low-income minority children and families who are displaced and excluded from the once vibrant communities that provided them with a sense of community, identity, and significant sources of cultural and social capital. Cucchiara (2008) has also shown that middle-class White families use their sense of privilege, power, and material resources to influence decisions that give advantage to their own children. The White families described by Cucchiara both implicitly and explicitly silenced and excluded low-income parents whose children were no longer able to gain access to magnet schools in newly gentrified areas. The result of this is that urban revitalization has the potential to create "new geographic patterns of opportunity and inequality, as schools become complicit in the creation of a 'dual city'" (Cucchiara, 2008, p. 176).

Researchers have for some time called attention to the social isolation that characterizes many high-poverty neighborhoods (e.g., Goldring, Cohen-Vogel, Smrekar, & Taylor, 2006). Drawing upon Wilson's (1987, 1996) theory of neighborhood effects, Stewart and her colleagues (2007) demonstrate that growing up in relative disadvantage—lacking, in particular, access to social capital, including role models and networks of information—affects children's aspirations significantly in spite of the possible mitigating circumstances of parents' involvement, both at home and at school, and the positive relationships that some students forge with their teachers. Even when parents and teachers serve as role models, their presence in children's lives may not be sufficient to balance out the lack of stable, consistent institutional support in school and access to material resources such as libraries. Moreover, these influences cannot always make up the difference for the lack of collective efficacy in neighborhoods based on trust and mutual responsibility, family income, level of food insecurity, or moves that families make over the course of children's school years (Berliner, 2014).

Yet others have explained that these neighborhoods have served as reservoirs of strength drawn from churches, families, neighborhood organizations, and friendships (e.g., Fullilove, 2004; Furstenberg et. al, 1999). In the end, Kinloch (2010), Haymes (1995), and others urge us to understand place as a "reality to be clarified and understood from the perspectives of the people who have given it meaning" (Tuan, 1979, p. 387). To do otherwise is to silence and marginalize the historical, cultural everyday meanings that people ascribe to place and cede the representation of urban space to a dominant narrative that diminishes the assets of low-income parents.

CONCLUSION

I began this chapter with the voices of parents who tell stories of how they support their children's education. Their stories serve as a counternarrative that disrupts the assumptions that many educators may have about parents' lack of skills, knowledge, and resources. I argue that if we define parent involvement narrowly as educators, then it's likely that we will not recognize or give legitimacy to parents' efforts to foster their children's learning. I focus on race and spatial inequality to emphasize the ways that power and privilege have not only reproduced inequality in schools, but have disenfranchised African American families who have long embraced the value of education. Still, I am optimistic that it is possible to forge meaningful partnerships with families that focus on the interests of children without succumbing to narrow conceptions of education. Children can flourish in a number of different ways, and much depends on providing them with the knowledge and tools they need to develop the capacity to participate fully as citizens in a democracy.

Unfortunately, changes in the political economy have hollowed out the core of cities, fragmented communities, and contributed to the unequal distribution of material resources. Together, Critical Race Theory and Critical Geography force us to examine the structural sources of inequality that have eroded public spaces and the common good in a racialized landscape that limits access to educational opportunities. Unfortunately, low-income families must shoulder the burden of a changing political economy in which they are often cast as consumers of education, rather than citizens whose children have a right to access quality schools. In the end, I stress spaces of hope as a way to describe a sense of community in which relationships, solidarity, and egalitarian values can flourish in public spaces. I also stress the ways that parents and families create spaces of hope that nurture relationships and children's capacities to learn, and prepare them for a flourishing life.

CHAPTER 2

The Power of Agency and Community at Ida B. Wells Primary School

When you're asking people to be involved it can't be something that is simply meeting your needs. . . . [Parents] have to be part of the process and their views have to be incorporated and appreciated. Communication should foster a cooperative relationship between the two stakeholders, you know, in the process of saying let us work together and, you know, what would you like to see happen, what would you like to have available for your child. What things can we do together and work on together.

—Administrator, Ida B. Wells

It seems like the teachers move them along so fast and nothing sinks in. . . . I feel like I teach them a lot more at home than anybody because I'm constantly at the dinner table with them or at their desk. And it seems like I had to reiterate everything they [were supposed to have] learned in class.

—Parent, Ida B. Wells

Parents' stories make visible the ways that they support and nurture their children's academic and emotional needs. Parents tell stories to inspire and motivate their children to do well in school. They create spaces in their homes where their children can read, discuss, and develop a sense of independence as learners. Moreover, parents recognize the challenges that their children face in school, where the process of learning is often a solitary act. Children are social and parents provide opportunities at home where they can be themselves. Children's voices, too, provide a window into the relationships they have developed with their parents and the joy they find in reading together. However, the parents whose stories I tell earlier do not necessarily feel at home at school. The spatial distance between home and school, both literal and ideological, reflects social inequalities, deficit theories, and mistrust.

The degree to which parents are a presence at school is a function of a school's willingness to recognize the intentional ways that parents are already involved and to discard dominant narratives that equate difference with deficit in reference to low-income families. Learning how to cross cultural and racial boundaries is essential to the ways in which educators train teachers, especially if the aim is to develop partnerships with families as a shared responsibility. Indeed, parents have to be part of the process, as the administrator at Ida B. Wells suggests above. However, it is one thing to say "let's work together"; it is quite another to ask whose interests parent involvement serves, who is accountable to whom, and whose knowledge counts in creating partnerships. These questions are significant in conceiving of ways to meet the needs of children who struggle to keep up with the pace of instruction and whose parents see a disconnect between home and school. In a culture of high-stakes testing, teachers feel the pressure to move forward with instruction and may not be able to fully gauge students' levels of comprehension and understanding. The parent above feels that she must "reiterate everything they [were supposed to have] learned in class." She takes on the role of teacher in helping her child. She feels that she is responsible. Otherwise her child will be left behind.

Unfortunately, parents have little hand in policies that affect their lives. Policies not only affect classroom instruction, but they affect where children go to school and parents' sense of community. This is particularly true of a local magnet school program, which has sought to attract more White families into the public schools, and the city's consent decree, which forced many children to leave their neighborhood schools. Devon, whose daughter attended Ida B. Wells, was disappointed with the changes he saw because he chose to send his daughter to Ida B. Wells, although he knew that the school had not achieved Annual Yearly Progress for the previous 4 years based on students' achievement on state tests. He was convinced that his daughter should go to school in the neighborhood where they lived and where they had a "faith home," even before his daughter had developed friendships with her classmates at Ida B. Wells. It's not surprising that parents like Devon are skeptical, ambivalent, and even hostile toward schools, particularly when they have chosen a school based on characteristics that are important to them.

Parents' concerns are not limited to the academic aspects of attending a given school. They also focus on relationships, community, family, a sense of belonging, and emotional well-being. Thus, it is crucial to ask whose interests parent involvement serves if, as educators, we are to address the complex needs that compete for parents' attention. After all, parents play many different roles in their relationships with their children, families, peers, and others in their community. Their roles shift depending on the context. At home, for example, they attend to their children's emotional needs, bolster their confidence, and teach their children to make decisions and create priorities about what is important in choosing friends, helping with family matters, and doing schoolwork. Parents also serve as advocates for their children to ensure that their children can participate in programs at the library, a community center, or clubs where children can be involved in enrichment activities that may not be readily affordable for many parents. The point is that parents are involved in addressing their children's needs in ways of which educators are often unaware. Parent involvement is simply not a given, but evolves in the context of social interaction to meet the demands of different situations.

Parents' shifting roles serve as a counternarrative that challenges the assumptions that many of us may hold about low-income families of color. As a participant-observer of parent meetings at Ida B. Wells (Appendix A), I learned that parents who attended these meetings were already involved by the ways they spoke about taking responsibility for their children's learning. They helped their children with their homework and created opportunities for learning at home and in the community. Many also recognized that learning is inextricably tied to teaching their children to be resilient, independent, faithful, moral individuals who need to be responsible for their own actions. Parent meetings created spaces within school where parents began to feel at home, where they began to hold teachers accountable, and where they shared their knowledge publicly with other parents and experts. I share their stories in the first part of this chapter (see Appendix C) and then describe the extent to which parent meetings provided a network of support that enabled parents to envision and enact different roles for themselves. They began to serve as advocates for their children at school by creating partnerships with teachers and administrators.

This chapter is a story of the principal's efforts to create a culture of parent involvement at Ida B. Wells, where she initially perceived little parent participation. By listening to parents' stories, she began to appreciate the role that parents played in their children's education. More than this, the principal relied on parents to more fully understand the value of collaboration. In her own words, she learned that partnerships are negotiated by grasping "the things we can do together and work on together."

PARENT INVOLVEMENT AT IDA B. WELLS

The story of Ida B. Wells began when the principal was disappointed with the scores of 2nd- and 3rd-graders on standardized tests. An African American woman who grew up in the neighborhood surrounding Ida

B. Wells, attended the school, and later taught there, the principal identified what she believed was one source of children's low performance: "If only parents were involved, I just know their children would do better in school." She was puzzled that parents did not ask her questions about why their children were not doing well. After all, she explained, the parents whose children flourished always wanted to know what more they could do to help their children. She wanted the families to know the value of holding high expectations, using literacy to forge relationships with their children, and gaining access to resources such as the library at school and cultural centers in the community to enhance children's learning.

The principal recalled vividly a not-so-distant time when families and teachers interacted at the school, the church across the street, and the grocery store down the block. These relationships are but a memory, as are many of the goods and services that were once a presence in the neighborhood, which served as a gathering place where parents and teachers greeted one another and could talk.

Built nearly 60 years ago in the art deco style, Ida B. Wells is set back about 100 feet from a busy thoroughfare that connects the northeast neighborhood to downtown. It's not uncommon to see children crossing this busy street in darkness when school begins, sometimes with a parent close behind, sometimes alone. Just to the north of Ida B. Wells is an angled road, a state highway that is one of the area's most frequently traveled intersections where high-speed traffic and congestion create hazardous conditions for pedestrians (St. Joseph County Housing Consortium, 2005).

The entrance to the school faces the neighborhood, where there is a park and neat rows of houses whose occupants live at or below the poverty line. However, according to a recent development plan, the surrounding neighborhood has been "vulnerable to negative economic and social forces, including White flight and slow economic growth." As the authors of this report explain, disparate commercial and residential structures show signs of "disinvestment" (www.ci.south-bend.in.us/sites/default/files/files/CED_CityPlan.pdf). Families near Ida B. Wells had limited access to goods and services, such as a full-service grocery store, pharmacy, health care providers, a library, employment opportunities, and reliable public transportation.

Beyond the busy intersection to the north and slightly west of Ida B. Wells is a neighborhood that city planners, the neighborhood association, and others have sought to rehabilitate (see Figure 2.1). Large single-family homes have begun to replace rental properties and vacant, deteriorating houses across a 60-acre section of land in the neighborhood. Older, cottage-style homes have been refurbished. Within sight of Ida B. Wells and directly to the north is a university and a once-impoverished neighborhood

Figure 2.1. Map of Area Surrounding Ida B. Wells

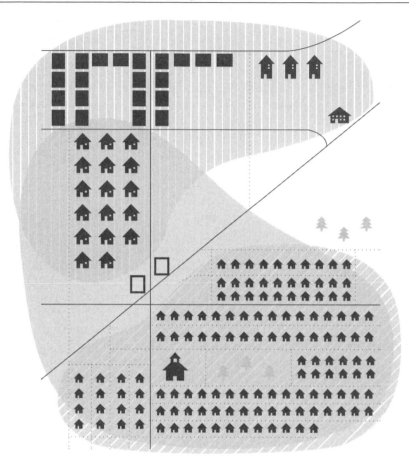

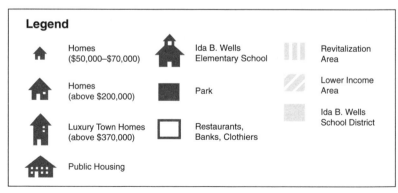

Legend

🏠 Homes ($50,000–$70,000)

🏠 Homes (above $200,000)

🏠 Luxury Town Homes (above $370,000)

🏠 Public Housing

🏫 Ida B. Wells Elementary School

⬛ Park

⬜ Restaurants, Banks, Clothiers

▥ Revitalization Area

▨ Lower Income Area

▨ Ida B. Wells School District

that now serves mostly White, high-income professionals who live in quarter-of-a-million-dollar condominiums and town houses and dine in upscale restaurants. The result of this neighborhood's transformation is a contradictory space of marginalized poverty and relative wealth—a spatially polarized landscape that epitomizes the core dynamics of racialized power and inequality here and in larger cities.

Aware of the economic constraints that limited parents' ability to participate at events at the school, the principal reflected on her own background of living in poverty. She did not realize until she was in high school that her father could not read, but he "knew he was responsible for his child's education. He knew he had to educate us in different ways. So, it had nothing to do with, you know, education at that time. I think it had something to do with maybe a belief system." Her family traveled because her father wanted her to accumulate experiences that would enhance her learning in school. These are the kinds of experiences that contribute to social and cultural capital, which her father recognized would help her achieve her goals as a future educator. Unfortunately, she was not confident that a new generation of parents values education and has made it a high priority: "I think just lack of education of what is needed. I don't think [parents] have been taught . . . from a child up that they are responsible for their child's education. It's not valued as a high priority." One could argue that the principal had initially internalized a dominant narrative that places blame on families for their children's poor performance in school. She also expressed the belief that families' engagement is really in the interests of schools (cf., Compton-Lilly, 2007): "Parent involvement is the foundation of children's learning. It's to support our teachers."

A SCHOOL-COMMUNITY-UNIVERSITY PARTNERSHIP

The principal's response to parents' "lack of involvement" was to reach out to university researchers, the director of a community literacy center, and other educators who formed the core of an education collaborative that met monthly for 2 years (see Appendix A). Her primary concern was to find ways to involve parents in school-sponsored events, and encourage them to attend parent-teacher conferences. She also wanted parents whose children were struggling in school to take a proactive approach to helping their children. With support from the education collaborative, the principal decided to create a space within the school where parents could have weekly conversations with one another and with teachers. The context of weekly meetings, or workshops, would also help parents build a network of support, share stories, and provide educators with an opportunity to learn from parents about their priorities, beliefs, values, and aspirations for their children. What started out as a one-semester, 12-week workshop became an ongoing series of workshops for 2 years in collaboration with another primary school.

Initially, the principal invited 25 families to participate in weekly parent meetings. She sent letters home, called, and visited homes to persuade families to attend workshops that focused on ways to support children's learning. These were families whose children were struggling in school, but the principal was convinced that the children could improve their performance in school if "parents were just more involved." As it turns out, 11 families, primarily African American, agreed to participate in the 1st year, and altogether 17 families participated during a period of 2 years. (See Appendix D for a profile of parents.) In keeping with Compton-Lilly's (2003) research, the principal and other participants agreed that before the principal developed any sort of curriculum for parent meetings, we should listen to parents' stories of growing up, going to school, and supporting their children.

With another researcher, I documented parents' and teachers' conceptions about what it meant to be "involved" (Greene & Long, 2010), and marked contrasts emerged. We learned from parents even before they attended meetings at the school that parents conceived of their role as supporting their children at home. They monitored their children's homework and helped when they could. They demonstrated that they were well aware of the challenges that their children faced in school and tried to compensate when instruction in school outpaced their children's development and understanding.

Listening to parents, the principal learned that it is important "to really embrace what parents are doing and then say here are some things I need for the school, you're gonna get them." This was a significant change from her earlier assumption that parents are not involved, that school is not a "high priority for them," or that the aim of parent involvement is to "support teachers." Further, she reflected, "Just because teachers don't see it doesn't mean it's not being done." Thus the principal sought to build on families' resources and create a dialogue that fostered mutual understanding.

We learned that parents' approaches to supporting and advocating for their elementary-aged children clustered around some common areas, and that stressed the extent to which parents are responsive to the needs of their children. For this initial group of 11 families, support manifested itself in the ways in which parents allowed their children space to make decisions and the extent to which they showed their children that they had choices. Importantly, giving their children this kind of space enabled parents to teach their children that the choices they made had consequences. Allowing children to have space may seem like a passive strategy, but parents who adopted such a view were mindful that they were teaching their children to become independent and self-reliant even at a young age. The same parents also provided hands-on help for their children with their schoolwork and guided their children with a clear understanding that they expected them to succeed in school. Thus parents cleared away distractions so that their children could do their homework as soon as they came home every afternoon.

At times, parents' support could be construed as advocacy. For example, home literacy (e.g., monitoring or helping with homework, reading together) is a form of support that can also be understood as a form of advocacy (i.e., acting on a child's behalf to gain advantage). One parent also spoke of doing research to find the best school for her child, relying on friends and family for advice before drawing her own conclusions about where to send her child. Identifying appropriate resources is a form of support that took her into the community, but not into the schools, to get the information she needed. In the end, many parents came to recognize the value of communicating with their children's teachers to clarify what teachers expected and to impress on teachers that they cared about their children's education.

In what follows, I describe the range of meanings that parents attached to supporting their children. My aim is to provide an inclusive view of parent involvement that focuses on parents' awareness, proclivities, and predispositions in adopting one role or another, not simply parents' behaviors or presence at school. Importantly, what I learned about parents' roles as supporters, and share here, I learned before parents participated in parent involvement workshops. Contrary to the dominant view of low-income African American parents as being detached or uninterested in their children's education, we learn here, and again in Chapter 4, that such parents actually approach their children's education with a sense of commitment and urgency. Parent meetings made visible the ways they already supported their children and may have created the conditions for parents' developing sense of agency in their efforts to advocate for their children. However, as I will detail later in the chapter, it is also significant that parents' efforts to reach out to educators were also met with resistance. As a result, parents' emerging sense of agency was very much a work in progress.

PARENTS AS SUPPORTERS

Monitoring and Helping with Homework

Parents' stories stressed the amount of time that family members spent monitoring their children's homework to ensure that their children completed their assignments with accuracy and precision. The routine for all of the parents was to tell their children to start their homework as soon as they came home from school. Most had created spaces in their homes with a desk and chair where their children could work quietly, but the lure of other children playing outside, video games, music, and television were distractions that could turn a 1-hour assignment into a 3-hour chore. One parent's description of getting her daughter started and then coming back to help was fairly typical of the challenges that parents faced: "As long as I was there, she could get everything done on that paper. But as long as I walked away she couldn't get anything done. So I make it a system. I'll help you read the directions and we'll do one and two but the rest has got to be on you. And then I'll come back and check stuff." A common refrain was that the children wanted to "just hurry up and get it done." The parents were well aware of their children's capabilities and were disappointed to see that they rushed through their homework so that they could do other things.

Evident from the very start of my conversations with parents was that the extent to which parents were involved and the role they constructed for themselves often depended on what their children needed at the time. As one parent put it, "You have to feel your children out." Parents typically adopted a hands-on approach to helping with homework by listening to their children read aloud, playing math games, or writing with their children if they saw that their children felt the work was too difficult or they did not understand the instructions. For example, Devon explained, "My daughter brought home some homework and I was looking at it this morning and she had missed like seven. She said these are new problems that are hard. I said, well I'll go through this and then we'll pick out the problem that you're having a hard time with and then I'll make up some problems for you and we'll go through 'em and get you going."

Similarly, another parent explained that she realized her daughter was having difficulties in school, and started to go to school with her daughter to motivate her: "I started getting a lot more involved about two years ago when Sonia felt like she was losing her motivation for school. She was seven. She was always excited about school. But then she started to lose her motivation. We didn't know what was behind it so I just started being at the school." This parent soon realized that her presence at school provided the motivation her daughter needed; in turn, her daughter's response to her mother's presence reinforced the reciprocal nature of parent involvement, with both parent and child influencing one another's actions: "I was excited about coming to the school and I was here all the time and I used to sit in class on test day and eat lunch with her and go to breakfast with her and whatever I can do because it seemed like the more excited I was the more excited she was." She was unemployed at the time, and used the opportunity she had to support her daughter. Unfortunately, most parents do not have the freedom to spend so much time at school with their children; hourly service jobs do not provide the flexibility that parents need in order to be a presence at school, particularly when hourly jobs extend into evenings and make it difficult for parents to attend PTA meetings and parent-teacher conferences.

Parents indicated that they were more aware of what was going on in school than many teachers might have given them credit for, especially with respect to their children's strengths and weaknesses, and whether or not schools were helping their children flourish. They seemed convinced that teachers were more concerned with covering the material than with their children's ability to understand the material. Reflecting the disconnect he felt, Devon explained, "I feel like I teach them a lot more at home than anybody because I'm constantly at the dinner table with them or at their desk. And it seems like I had to reiterate everything they learned." Devon observed that "the way the schools are set up, they're rushing them so fast. Like, Michelle was doing addition and then they were introducing subtraction but she hadn't mastered addition and then they moved on to multiplication and she still wasn't okay with the addition." Teachers often operate under a level of stress in a climate of increased standards, accountability, and testing. A focus on outcomes can also negate the rhythms of students' learning and the kind of teaching that follows children's developmental paths in culturally relevant ways.

Listening and Building Children's Self-Esteem

I listened to parents who explained the ways they responded to their children's needs by helping to build their self-esteem. For example, Marc's efforts were directed at helping his six boys believe in themselves and persist: "I try to teach 'em don't ever give up. Whatever you do don't give up because there's somebody somewhere that can help you with whatever it is that you need help with. If you're not getting it, if I can't help you, we'll find somebody that can help you, and I'll do that. And I think that's important." Similarly, Amy tried to be a model for her children and worked tirelessly to help her youngest, who attends Ida B. Wells, develop confidence despite a slight speech impediment: "I have to constantly encourage her that, you know, that's just part of who you are, don't let that discourage you from anything, you read just as well as the next person, so I have to push her a little bit more than some of the other kids." Her efforts to create a learning space for her daughter existed apart from any encouragement at school.

Amy recognized the needs of children in the neighborhood and reached out to nurture them in ways that contrasted with her own experiences of growing up. Such an approach also supported her daughter's learning and created a social network among a group of four single mothers who could rely on one another for help, including day care and some supervision for academic work.

> We sit all the kids down in a room and we pass around a chapter book and everybody has to read a page, and if you're a good reader and you're sitting by one of the younger kids, then you have to help them sound out the words very patiently, very kindly, very lovingly, not talking down to them.

Amy learned to create what I would describe as a learning community—modeled not on her own mother, but on one of the foster families she grew up in. In fact, her mother often intimidated her and fueled her insecurities as a reader. She also explained a significant source of her commitment to others: "I grew up in a single-parent home and I made myself a promise that no matter what [we go through] if I'm there or not that my kids will never go through it. I know how hard it is being a single parent. Most kids that grow up in broken homes aren't really successful."

Parents' efforts to be involved and foster their children's learning occurred within the context of children's interests and sense of identity. As one parent put it, "It depends on where that kid's at, you know, you know all your kids and where they are at, so you know to discipline 'em on different things, so some things is good and some things is bad, so every parent know their kid." Another emphasized the value of finding different ways to support children in ways that reflected what they believed their children needed: "You kinda have to feel your children out, when one thing won't work for 'em, don't give up on 'em, find another avenue." All of the parents attending parent meetings seemed to understand the importance of listening to their children and establishing an emotional bond through conversation.

This sense of "finding different ways," "disciplining them," and "find[ing] another avenue" challenges assumptions that some researchers have about low-income families' involvement. For example, Lareau (2003) has characterized low-income and working-class families as inattentive to their children's needs, arguing that they rely on a "natural growth" model of parent involvement in contrast to the strategies of "concerted cultivation" that middle-class families use. However, the binary that Lareau (2003) creates is misleading. I would argue that the distinction is more fluid than she would allow, given the proactive strategies for responding to their children that the working-class parents describe above.

Providing Children with Room to Become Independent Learners

Parents recognized that they needed to support their children in strategic, intentional ways, but they also took a hands-off approach. For example, Beatrice emphasized the necessity of giving her children support in life and space to learn by making sure they were aware that their decisions had consequences:

> They can keep each other company and do their own little thing when they want to. They can have their space when they want to. I think the biggest thing is, I just make my kids deal with the consequences of their actions. I mean, let them make decisions that some people feel like at that age they shouldn't make, but you know what, you're going to have to deal with the consequences, you might as well let them know at a young age because you're going to have to do it all your life.

This type of life lesson applied to what she tried to teach her children about school and the intrinsic motivation she wanted them to develop in making the right decisions. She offered this rationale for her approach: "You're going to have to sit there and get it done anyway, you know? On his own, my son is going to have to say, 'I'm going to do my homework because I don't want to have after-school detention,' instead of me sitting here, you know, giving him the answers and doing it for him."

Beatrice also provided structure to help her children see that she was committed to supporting their education. Mirroring Amy's approach, Beatrice gathered her children around a "big giant dining room table" and relied on her children to help out one another: "If they need help go get your brother or sister I mean, you know and it teaches them how to take care of each other and look out for one another so when they get older, you know they already watch out for one another. They've got that bond." Therese took a similar approach by providing her children with the space they needed to work independently on their homework, although her work schedule and her husband forced the issue: "I come home or when they see me and, you know, to show me their homework, after they're done I'll go over it, and then after that they're pretty much just go do their own thing. Then their dad gets up, because I work in the evening. When they're home from school I basically go to work." Despite Therese's seemingly hands-off approach to supporting her children, she cared for and nurtured them. She read to her youngest daughter when she could and expected her older children to help one another with their schoolwork.

Serving as a Role Model

Parents' awareness was not limited to school-based assignments. Like other parents, Keisha explained that she "pushed" all of her children to succeed. "I kinda give them my story and that kinda make 'em go a little further, kinda give 'em inspiration." Marc, whose background was, in his own words, "hard," also expressed the importance of serving as a role model for his children—especially as an African American father. Having grown up in a single-parent family with a strong mother, he wanted to be a presence in his sons' lives. "I can only do the best I can do," he explained. "I try to give my children what I didn't have." He wanted his sons to have an "affinity for others' well-being" and a strong sense of faith. Therefore, he expected them to contribute to the local community: "We had them see what the homeless shelter looks like. We let them serve food on Christmas, you know. We take baskets around to people who don't have food. You kind of got to have them see the world for what it is. So, that's our system." Providing his sons with experiences such as working in a homeless shelter or delivering meals to people reflected Marc's commitment to building his sons' character. He wanted his sons to be kind and care about others even if they are facing their own struggles.

Marc taught his children "morals, values, you know, what's important, what's false, what's true, that's something that I'm working on." After all, he explained that it was "important to teach kids, and some people don't, but I think it is because I mean you always, as a parent you always want your children to do a little bit better than you've done. I mean, at least I do." Norton (2010) argues that it can be quite easy to ignore the ways in which children and their families use faith to develop a sense of strength needed to transform seemingly painful situations into opportunities for spiritual growth, adequacy, and direction in their lives (see also Comer, 2004). It is also important to understand how parents and their children move in and out of multiple spaces. Participating in events at church or a local homeless shelter shed light on the ways that families help their children develop a sense of place, identity, and belonging.

In addition, Marc explained how he reached out to others to instill in other youth the values that he has embraced and that he taught his children. Like two other fathers who participated in parent meetings, he was aware that "guys that have children that's totally just abandoned." Therefore,

> I'm a mentor at a middle school. I've mentored this student who's in the 6th grade. This is a really wonderful experience for me to kind of tap into another, you know, just another youth, another youth and invest some, maybe some positive things that I may be able to interject and, you know, just sit back and read with him, spend time and then tell him what I tell my own boys, that you're something, you're going to do something great one day.

He was committed to helping African American youth focus on their education and flourish. In addition, he wanted to give back to a community that helped him, especially Habitat for Humanity, which built the house that he lived in with his six boys, his nephew, and his wife of 11 years.

Building Resilience, Creating Hope

Like many of the parents who participated in workshops, Marc said that he was trying to survive. "We're like, okay, how do we survive, how do we survive in a society with the economics just crashing down and just from going to work and coming home to a house filled with eight people." In doing so, he taught his children that they mattered. This was exemplified at the fellowship dinners they all attended at church, his presence at the sporting events in which they participated, or the free piano lessons he secured for his son.

Amy's words echoed Marc's. Amy taught her children to persist in the face of the struggles they have experienced:

> We need to struggle together [rather] than everybody trying to pull their separate ways. I try to be honest with my kids, you know, this is where we're at and this is what we're going through and this is what we gotta do to get to the other side, and you know, when we lived in those projects I would tell 'em, you know, I know it's really crampy in here and I know it's just, I said but you know what, this is just a stepping-stone. This isn't the end, you know, each time it'll get better.

Amy could not help but draw upon a wellspring of hope that helped her get though high school while taking care of an infant and maintaining an apartment. She taught her children important lessons about surviving together as a family.

Creating Safe Spaces

Finally, parents told many stories about supporting their children by protecting them in a neighborhood where both economic and educational policies fragmented any real sense of community. Like other parents participating in the study, Maya spoke of protecting her children and creating a "safe" place. She grew up with her aunt, a brother, and her cousins after her mother and sister were murdered. Maya lived near Ida B. Wells, but she has not been able to escape the violence of the city in which she grew up or the social isolation that fear brings about:

> It's a good neighborhood but it's the people in the neighborhood, it's like it's dark down there and then they work their way down here where it's good, and it's sometimes I'm scared to let my kids play outside 'cause last summer right at the corner somebody was shooting at somebody and I'm like should I let my kids go outside, or should I make 'em stay in the house.

Latrisse, too, lived in a neighborhood close to Ida B. Wells. Her main concern was that few children her sons' age lived near them. She was equally concerned about the amount of drug activity that they saw on their way to school. Unemployed for 3 years, she was able to accompany her youngest son to school, but not all of the parents had that luxury and worried about their children walking on narrow sidewalks alongside a busy corridor to downtown. The high-traffic area near the school was particularly worrisome for parents in the winter, when few people cleared the sidewalks and children would be forced to walk in the street.

Devon walked with his daughter to Ida B. Wells Primary School, and his reflections at the outset of this chapter underscore the challenge of staying connected to other families:

> So you're not involved, you know, you don't have that close-knit relationship like when I went to school. Everybody knew their kids 'cause they all went to the same school. Here you be on one street, another street and kids going over here and they got a line of kids waiting for this bus to go that way and stuff. Totally messed up.

Devon's comments called attention to the result of creating magnet schools in the city, which forced many students to leave their neighborhood schools. In addition, the city's consent decree had some negative effects because minority students could be bused across the city to help ensure some degree of racial balance. These efforts at racial balancing failed and, by some measures, over 30% of the 10 primary schools in this city were actually out of compliance (Warlick, 2011). Devon felt little connection to a school that once served as the center of his neighborhood. Similarly, Therese spoke of the value of neighborhood schools: "Everything's changed so much now with the districts and everything, you could live across the street from somebody and they'll go to a different school." If parents believe decisions that affect their children are beyond their control, they may be unsure about how to take on significant roles that connect home and school. Although policy-makers may not recognize that decisions in education or economic development can isolate low-income families, the districting policies in the neighborhood surrounding Ida B. Wells are a clear example.

For example, Paviel reflected on how the city's redevelopment of the area between Ida B. Wells and the university has affected her.

> It's really not the same as what it used to be because before a lot of people are no longer in the neighborhood. That's what makes it so different . . . It's had its share of problems but I never knew of any big problems. But a lot of people that were in this neighborhood, in this area, have been they've died, gone to jail, moved on . . . They're being pushed out of the neighborhood because they're buying up everything.

Paviel's words explain how the displacement that has fragmented the neighborhood where she lives produces inequality, as investors focus on new gentrified spaces and disinvest in low-income neighborhoods. This is a significant factor, since researchers studying parent involvement underscore the value of parents developing relationships with diverse groups of people who can potentially broaden their understanding of how to support their children's education. Likewise, Stanton-Salazar (1997) has described this as a "social networks framework," which explains the ways in which social networks can both impede and foster access to a number of opportunities: namely, advocacy, role models, emotional and moral support, advice, and guidance. Access to these networks can easily determine which students can make it and which cannot.

PARENTS AS ADVOCATES

I use the term *advocacy* here to describe an emerging set of strategies that parents learned over time as a means for gaining opportunity for their children in school. One way that parents advocated for their children was to actively find the best school or program for a child. For example, Therese initially wanted her children to attend the primary school where she had gone to school as a child. However, she spoke with friends and family and recognized why she should send them to a school with programs tailored to her children's needs: "They had a nice teacher over there but to me, over here [Ida B. Wells], they have more programs to help, they been working with [my son] so much." She also enrolled her son in a summer program at a local community center and "the [family coordinator] she's really been working with my kids." By the time parents started to attend parent meetings, Ida B. Wells had missed the cutoff for Annual Yearly Progress for 4 consecutive years. As a consequence, all parents received a notice that explained that they had the option to send their children to another school or receive supplemental services such as the one Therese sent her son to. None chose the former and about half chose the latter.

A second way that parents advocated for their children was to meet with teachers to rectify a problem. Parents were well aware of the problems that many of their children faced in school, ranging from not turning in assignments to simply not being able to keep up with the pace of instruction. Damian explained that he was trying to be as proactive as possible because he believed that "the teachers can be excellent if the parent is there to aid and assist the teacher. If the parent is not there to assist the teacher, then [some teachers, but not all] tend to let the child go, which is unfortunate. But I see now that the teachers have so much to deal with."

However, few parents were a presence at school or took proactive steps to speak to a teacher until after they began to meet teachers in the workshops they attended. In that context, teachers spoke to parents about their expectations for completing homework and explained ways the parents could help their children with both math and reading. At the same time, parents had the opportunity to tell teachers the problems they had with some of the assignments that their children had difficulty completing. The parents explained that few assignments were accompanied by instructions, so that they could not really help their children with the homework teachers sent home. Teachers were listening and parents understood that what they said mattered.

Parent meetings broadened the scope of people within the realm of their children's education with whom the parents interacted. This network of people included teachers at Ida B. Wells, administrators, the art educator at a local museum, community members, and other parents. Finding that other parents shared the same challenges contributed to parents' ability to imagine different ways they could be engaged in their children's education. These increased interactions changed the ways they applied their knowledge, skills, and resources in order to help themselves and their children thrive. Indeed, families repeatedly spoke about the ways in which they were relying on one another for advice, support, and inspiration to help their children flourish. Marc explained that Richard motivated him to "stay on task" with his children, even when he was tired after working all day. No longer were parents as isolated in their efforts to help their children. Parents reminded one another, "If you are going to change, then you need to make sacrifices."

That parents could rely on one another and on the principal helped encourage parents' emerging sense of agency and capacity for making changes in their children's lives at school. A key turning point for parents occurred when the principal gave all of the participants their children's test scores. Therese's youngest son placed in the lowest percentile, even though his grades in class placed him in "honors." She was stunned, recalling "and that opened [my] eyes to look around, look around us and see, and pay attention to how the kids are doing." Therese reiterated this story at a regional meeting of researchers studying the effects of poverty on families that she attended with me at a local literacy center near Ida B. Wells:

> When I realized that my kids were slipping in school, I knew that it
> was my responsibility, not only my child's teachers' responsibility, to
> help them learn. So when I see low test scores, okay I realize I got to
> do something about it. Therefore I got to check book bags. I wasn't
> checking book bags like I was supposed to. I visit their teachers
> and see how they're doing in class, see how things are going in the
> classroom, what they're struggling with, things like that. And now
> we're [with her husband] building a relationship with the school and
> the teachers.

Therese's reflections illustrated the extent to which parents can defer to schools when they believe teachers have their children's best interests at heart. However, Therese developed the capacity to intervene on her children's behalf at school. She entered her children's schools with a growing sense of empowerment and accepted her more active role by holding all of her children's teachers accountable. More than this, presenting her story at a meeting of researchers revealed her emerging role as an advocate for her own and other's children.

Richard also saw his son's test scores as a betrayal of his trust because he believed his son was doing well:

> I didn't have certificates hanging on my refrigerator saying he's an
> honor roll student, but like every report he got honor roll, but the

test scores were so low how he could be a honor roll student. I didn't understand that, and I never will understand it.

Richard had difficulty reconciling his son's performance at school with his perception of his son's intelligence at home: "I know at home he's very intelligent. I know he has it, he has the potential to learn. He even tells me he wants to learn." Richard assumed that his son's teacher knew his son was struggling given the evidence of his son's test scores. If his son's teacher knew, it was clear that she did not explain ways that Richard could help.

Like Therese, Richard had begun to feel more at home at school after attending parent meetings. He made a conscious effort to become more active at school by creating relationships with all of his sons' teachers. At a school district-wide meeting, Richard led a session called Parents Talking to Parents. He emphasized the value of persistence and communication with teachers. He found that his children's teachers were not always responsive to his overtures to talk about his children's progress, but he emphasized for parents at this session the importance of "staying on" teachers. In large part, his vigilance was prompted by his lack of trust in schools' ability to ensure his sons' success.

In the session on Parents Talking to Parents, which he cochaired with Therese, Richard described telling a teacher that he wanted to know how one of his sons was progressing. However, at the end of an 8-week grading period, Richard went to meet his son's teacher and found out that his son was not doing well. Richard's response was to tell the teacher, "You are going to communicate with me, and you're gonna listen to me. And once he knew that I meant what I said, now we communicate. He probably calls once a week now. Because he knows that I care about what my son is doing in school." Richard gave voice to the sense of purpose—if not their frustration—that other parents felt in their own efforts to talk with teachers and helped empower others to advocate for their children in a very public realm.

Parents' growing knowledge of how to navigate the institution of school helped them to gain advantage for their children. As in Barton's study (Barton et al., 2004), parents began to acquire new forms of capital that included their ability to "question school policy," affirm "the validity of their concerns," and create a space for engaging in their children's education. Nonetheless, parents' strategies for advocacy were, to use Auerbach's (2007) words, "still under construction." Their efforts were at times rebuffed, and many of the children still struggled in school despite parents' increased presence at school. However, these facts do not take anything away from parents' roles as advocates.

PARENT-SCHOOL-COMMUNITY PARTNERSHIPS

In this chapter, I have focused on one principal's efforts to reach out to families and, in the end, work together with these families to help children flourish. She was able to persuade a number of families to participate in workshops by visiting them at home. She attended all of the workshops, she listened to parents who felt that the school misled them when their children were placed on the honor roll in their classes but then they failed to reach grade level on standardized tests, she acknowledged and praised the ways in which parents sought to educate their children in the broadest sense of the word, and she assured them that she valued their contribution to this joint venture when she asked them to serve as mentors for other parents whose children attended Ida B. Wells.

Although the principal began with the assumption that increasing family engagement would support teachers, the unintended consequence over a 2-year period was the strong sense of community that began to develop among the small cohort of families she invited to participate in these workshops. This sense of community helped to create conditions for agency and capacity, particularly family members' ability to consider alternative futures for their children, to get access to resources, and to hold accountable those who were in power.

By focusing on parents' and children's lived experiences, I have sought to go beyond models that focus on the needs of schools in order to understand parents' values and aspirations for their own children. By identifying parents' values and aspirations, I underscored the ways that parent involvement served the interests of parents and children and the extent to which accountability for parent involvement rested on parents' beliefs and priorities. Emphasizing parents' own needs is a significant point of departure from models that make parents accountable to schools (e.g., (Epstein, 2010) and raises questions about what counts as parent involvement. Listening to parents' voices also helps us see the extent to which what matters most to families is often not visible to educators. Parents did not limit their involvement to supporting their children's performance on standardized test scores, but adopted a broad conception of education. In the end, parents offered a view of education that serves as a model for teachers. Such a model embraces the joy of learning, collaboration, patience, compassion, care, civic engagement, community, and family.

As others have also suggested (e.g., Graue & Hawkins, 2010), it is important that educators understand more fully who parents are, what parents are already doing to support their children, and develop models of parent involvement that are reciprocal and collaborative. As I mention in the introductory chapter to *Race, Community, and Urban Schools*, not all parents are like those who participated in parent meetings or have access to the resources I describe. Therefore, reciprocity requires that educators balance their own goals and expectations with parents' beliefs, values, and priorities. Such a view is dialogic and requires that parents and educators listen respectfully to one another in order to collaborate in the best interests of children whose development is not linear but follows the contours of their interactions in multiple contexts.

However, parent involvement alone cannot create more equitable conditions for low-income families of color whose children struggle in school or who lack access to significant material resources to help their children flourish. Within the conditions of relative social isolation parents were limited by policies that seemed to work against the very conditions that can enable children to flourish. For example, the school corporation's efforts to create racial balancing called attention to the power and privilege that can take children away from their neighborhoods and fail to provide them with a safe, nurturing environment to learn and go to school. Some parents made explicit their awareness that something was changing in their neighborhoods that worked against the sense of community they valued. Nonetheless, these same parents did not attribute their current circumstances or the roles they played in their children's education to living in poverty, to policy, or to race. One could argue that parents have internalized a dominant narrative that emphasizes personal responsibility and the extent to which education alone has the potential to change their children's life paths (Compton-Lilly, 2007). One could also argue that parents did not have access to a privileged discourse about market forces. However, a changing political economy has indeed eroded a "firewall of protection" (Hacker & Pierson, 2010) against an unequal distribution of wealth manifested in the racial landscape of urban neighborhoods surrounding Ida B. Wells. Indeed, nearly one in three children lives in poverty in the city where parent meetings took place and at least one in five experiences food insecurity; both statistics exceed national averages (Coordinating Committee of the Community Forum for Economic Development, 2012).

All things being equal, parents aspire to live in neighborhoods where their children will be safe and have access to quality schools, libraries, well-lit parks with fields and other facilities, and programs where they can create social networks with other adults who can help supervise their children. These social networks are significant since they create cultural capital and help children and families increase their chance for social mobility. As Sangha (2013) puts it, "The more people bump into one another, the more ingrained a family becomes into a community and the more information that [families can] exchange." Sangha tells the story of one parent who, in trying to get access to educational programs, spends time at the park just to get what this parent referred to as the "playground gossip." Unfortunately, things are not equal and the decisions that parents at Ida B. Wells made about where to live reflected a bigger picture that affected the roles they played in negotiating risk and opportunity. Thinking spatially about the ways in which children come into contact with people (e.g., peers and adults) and institutions (e.g., educational, commercial, civil, social) throws into relief the limits that are placed on children from low-income families of color. Moreover, policies that determine where parents live and where their children go to school are often beyond their control.

With little commitment for any comprehensive economic development in urban neighborhoods, policy efforts can be directed toward developing social capital and creating networks of support to ensure that families have access to resources. For example, Amy's ability to create a learning community with other parents reflected a valuable source of social capital, or what Sampson and his colleagues (2002) described as "collective efficacy." Collective efficacy derives from "mutual trust and shared expectations" in neighborhoods where parents such as Amy intervene in the interests of the "public good" (p. 457). Schools and communities can work together to build on assets that parents bring by increasing parents' capacity for developing the well-being of a neighborhood and the grounds for social action. Similarly, Marc offered a model of a home-school-community partnership based on his ethic of service, his work with young men of color, and his commitment to giving back to the community that provided his family with a home. Indeed, he helped us to see the many spaces where learning can occur and the ways in which parents can become teachers who give children meaning in their lives.

The cultivation of social capital can facilitate a degree of empowerment when parents become partners, decision-makers, and collaborators with schools and provide a necessary sense of accountability and control. Parents can also become examples to their children of how to participate in the political process in order to advocate for distributing resources equitably. Leveraging human capital can, in turn, provide the basis for economic development that will "transform the character and quality of life of urban areas" (Noguera, 2001, p. 198). Parents and community organizations can marshal resources (information, legal aid, financial and job counseling) and expand their social networks with other supportive organizations, such as churches, businesses, non-profits, and established civic groups. This expanding social capital can create power to leverage change in schools, so that they more effectively meet the needs of the children and families they serve.

CONCLUSION

As educators, we can explore both the visible and not-so-visible markers of difference to complicate what we know and what we think we know about the families whose children we teach. Part of reaching out to families is also about teachers inviting families into the classroom as much as possible to learn about what they value and recognize what they want for their children. Allen (2007, 2010) affirms the value of using families' "funds of knowledge" as resources that can help children flourish. Memoirs, other types of writing, photographs, and even iMovies can facilitate partnerships that support children. She has also suggested that teachers walk through neighborhoods to understand firsthand where and how families live and to grasp the lived experiences of families both culturally and racially (Ordoñez-Jasis & Flores, 2010).

What is not clear for parents are the roles that educators want them to play. As we learn more about what parents are already doing on behalf of their children, what additional roles do we want parents to play? If parents could be more of a presence at school, how much space are we willing to create for parents to facilitate joint collaboration and decision-making? How can teachers and parents create partnerships to ensure that children have access to what they need in the many spaces where they have opportunities to learn?

In the next chapter, I place children's stories at the center of ongoing conversations about parent involvement and the roles that parents play in their children's academic and emotional lives at home, in school, and in the community. Children's stories make visible the reciprocal, caring relationships between children and their families that often go unnoticed in studies of parent involvement.

CHAPTER 3

"We're Spending Time Together"
What We Can Learn from Children About Parent Involvement

With Maureen McQuillan

"We will go to the library and then we will get out some books."

"She'll read the question about the book and then I have to study it first, and then we answer the questions together."

"She said when I grow up and get my education you could set your mind on being whatever you want to be."

"We're spending time together and he's helping me, and that just feels good because some people don't have parents that are there to help them."

The children's voices above are 5th- and 6th-graders who describe the ways in which their parents are involved in their learning. Parents accompany them to the library, help them comprehend the stories they read, encourage them with high expectations, and just spend time with them. This time together gives children a sense of belonging, self-worth, and value, particularly when they need reassurance and confidence in the face of challenging circumstances.

Parents' stories in Chapter 2 reveal the roles that parents play in their children's lives and the extent to which they respond to their children's emotional and academic needs. Children's recollections in this chapter also serve as a window into the ways their parents support learning, but, in addition, provide glimpses into the experiences that are meaningful to children and the advice on which they act (see Appendix E). For instance, we learned from Paige in the introductory chapter that she valued the intimacy of reading *Raising a Dragon* with her mother before going to sleep, the time they spent together at the library looking "stuff up" on the computer, or the evenings her mother and father helped her with her homework. At an early age, Paige's parents fostered their daughter's identity as a reader with a bright future. When she was in 4th grade, Paige told a story of the time 3 years earlier when she carried an armful of books with her mother at her side to the checkout counter at the public library. The librarian asked quizzically if she was really going to read all of those books. Paige met the librarian's question with a report on all of the books she had read and just returned. The librarian became her friend and often looked for books that she knew Paige would enjoy reading. Although not an avid reader, Paige's mother told Paige, "If I feel like I wanted to read then that's what I should do. Um, set my mind on reading books." She spoke with pride about the library in her room. "I collect a lot of books," Paige once explained.

At the outset of *Race, Community, and Urban Schools*, we also learn from Jada the extent to which places embed memories and serve to nurture children's imaginative and emotional lives. Jada and her cousin often read together in the upstairs closet at home where they could experience some quiet moments. With flashlights, snacks, and books in hand, they squeezed themselves tightly together in a quiet space apart from the adult conversations downstairs. At the same time, Jada's face also lit up when she spoke of the moments when she and her mother read together in her mother's bedroom. More often than not, however, she spent time at her aunt's house (her "Teetee") because Jada's mother worked, or her aunt and cousin would come to Jada's house after school. Her aunt often provided a meal after Jada and her cousin finished their homework at the kitchen table. By her own description, Jada was a confident student who once explained, "I'm smart. I can help people with their work and like if people don't want to do their work I can help them go over it, just like my mom and my Teetee showed me how to do it." Not unlike Paige, Jada had developed a sense of confidence and independence derived from a strong sense of family who believed in her capacity as a learner and provided a great deal of social support.

In both cases, Paige and Jada learn to be resourceful, to rely on themselves, and to study. We also learn from both girls that their parents were vigilant about their daughters' surroundings, echoing the concerns expressed by parents in Chapter 2 who were troubled by the erosion of a sense of community and increased violence in neighborhoods, the latter of which the city continued to ignore. The children, too, were fearful of the strangers who sit in front of abandoned houses and talk to them on their way home from school. Their parents gave them phones so they can tell them where they are and call if there is an emergency. If she was not working, Jada's mother accompanied her daughter to the park. Jada once explained that her mother often sat in her car and watched her daughter play. Both Jada and Paige were afraid to walk in parks alone where the equipment is old, rusted, and in disrepair.

In the remainder of this chapter, I detail four children's perceptions of their parents' involvement at home, at school, and in the community over a period of 3 years. When I first met these four children, they were least two standard measures below grade level in reading. I center the voices of children as a way to tell the stories of the different ways that African American families—parents, grandparents, aunts, and siblings—support and advocate for children. As I mention in the Introduction, their voices constitute what my colleagues and I have called the Adult-Child Imaginary (Greene, Burke, & McKenna, 2013) to explain the seemingly innocent ways that children convey meaning—in this case, the meaning of their parents' involvement. We learn from children some conventional wisdom about the ways in which their parents are involved, from reading aloud from children's favorite books while sitting beside them to helping with homework and meeting with their teachers. Some of the information we learn we can acquire from parents themselves. However, children's stories reveal the power of intimacy that exists between children and their families, particularly those moments when they share stories sheltered from the stresses of children's day-to-day lives at school, in their neighborhoods, and sometimes at home. Children describe the approaches that their parents take to help them with homework, the expectations parents convey when they encourage their children to do well in school, and the extent to which parents create spaces where their children can flourish academically, emotionally, and spiritually. In turn, the children's stories become part of a collective narrative that illustrates the ways that parents are invested in their children's lives in the disinvested spaces of deteriorating neighborhoods.

By taking the long view of parent involvement over time, I have tried to capture the changing circumstances of children's lives (see also Compton-Lilly, 2007, 2012). Some children grow increasingly independent over time and have confidence that they know a subject well enough not to seek their parents' help. Indeed, as we saw in Chapter 2, parents often give their children that space. However, as children grow older, they face new emotional and intellectual challenges. Their identities change relative to their relationships to different family members, their teachers, and their peers. As I show in this chapter, they may very well need their parents' support to navigate the change over time. Such a perspective sheds light on the extent to which parents respond to their children's developmental and emotional needs.

Importantly, children's stories can help us understand the kinds of relationships that are necessary to help support children's sense of self-esteem and resilience. As Smagorinsky (2012) has pointed out, students' positive emotional outlook can fuel their sense of confidence and enable them to approach challenges with a belief that they can solve a given problem and to persist when their initial efforts may very well frustrate them. Children can also point to the reasons why we might be losing children's attention in school and highlight areas where we could potentially make learning more personally meaningful and significant.

PAIGE: "BOOKS SOOTHE ME"

Paige's narrative brings into focus the extent to which parent involvement is often part of a network of peers, family members, and educators. Paige learned to rely on different people at different times, although her parents' support was both consistent and profound. She could turn to them when she was most in need of their help. The nature and quality of their relationship with Paige was what stood out more than how much they were involved.

At the time I was writing, Paige was 12 years old and in 6th grade. She lived with her mother and father in a modest house and she had a close relationship to her aunt, cousins, and grandmother. She also had a supportive circle of friends with whom she was close. They often came over to say hello whenever I spoke with Paige in the school cafeteria. Teachers and children alike knew and respected her. She also seemed to have developed a very positive relationship with a special education teacher who worked with her cousin. Paige liked talking with him and wanted "to be close to [her] teachers so [she could] just go and talk to them about personal stuff at home and just talk." She would "like it if teachers knew her" and they "could get to know each other."

Paige explained that she loved school from the time I first spoke with her in 4th grade. After all, she said "when I'm a student, we get to do special things and we can come to school to be with our friends and stuff." However, she then qualified her remark when she said, "I only got one friend out of this whole school." By this, she meant that she had only one peer who loved school the way she did. She had begun to develop an identity as a good student consistent with what her teacher and her parents expected from her, but she was also aware that other students resented her. Still, she seemed to accept what others felt without any resentment. In fact, she seemed self-assured in her efforts to be a good student and forge a relationship with a friend who "likes doing the same things. . . . Like most of the kids in my class, they don't like doing math and me and her like doing math and we like doing stuff like when the teacher tell [sic] us we're doing something, all the students get mad, but me and her, we are doing it." Paige expressed her confidence and belief in herself when she affirmed in 4th grade that she couldn't let others' opinions influence her.

Based on many conversations with her parents and others in her family, Paige seemed to have already developed a single-mindedness about why school was important. For her, confidence was "Like don't give up . . . believe in what you're doing like if somebody tells you you're not going to make it, like to college, you don't let that get into your head. You try your best and try to live your dream like, 'cause . . . before you do anything you got to go to school." Indeed, her father had told her "to never give up, you just got to do good in school and pay attention and listen." By 5th grade, she reiterated why she loved school when she said, "I'm learning new stuff," and had gown popular in what was becoming a wide circle of friends who she referred to as her "sisters." We are "like sisters because if we see another one of my friends . . . we try to make them happy, so they won't be like mad . . . I don't like seeing none of my friends mad. It just ruins their day and my day, too." The way Paige's mother nurtured her seems to have carried over into the relationships that Paige established with her friends; friendships have become an extension of Paige's already large family.

Paige's family animated her love of stories and shaped her identity as a reader and writer more than any other factor. Paige often recounted the Sunday morning breakfasts that she shared with her mother, father, aunt, and cousins: "We talk and share some family stories about when [her mother] was little." Similarly, she reflected on the walks that she took with her family near her school. "We come to our school and just look at the river or take a walk by the river." Asked about the best part of the river, Paige said, "Sharing memories and talking about feelings and how the day went and, um, because my little cousin, she just turned four, and she tells, like, crazy stories about how she and how last night I went to a princess castle and she said I was a princess and I caught a dragon." Story was at the heart of Paige's family, along with words and imagination.

Ultimately, Paige's family helped explain her love of reading and how Paige used reading to make sense of her feelings and her surroundings. Her mother encouraged her to read and helped build the collection of books in Paige's library at home. The sheer number and variety of books that Paige had read was nearly as impressive as her recollection of the details of what she read. Importantly, for Paige, reading was a means for learning. For example, after reading *Kate Forever*, she explained that she "just got on the computer and just started looking up stuff and then I just start reading it." In 6th grade, she identified *Number the Stars* as one of her favorite books and Bluford Books, including *The Test* and *Pretty Ugly*. She also loved talking about *Frank the Mighty, Holes, Hidden Children, Stolen Children, Until We Meet Again, Room in the Attic,* and *Tuck Everlasting*. She read these books on her own, not for class, and frequently read with her cousin in the quiet of her bedroom.

For Paige, books served to awaken her imagination and she could easily become one of the characters with whom she identified. More poignantly, however, Paige learned to read as a means of quieting her soul. The stress of school, especially testing, the trauma of losing her grandfather in 5th grade, the fights at school, and the lack of safe spaces, kept her from just being a kid. So at times, she read to learn about the ways that the characters she admired came to terms with the struggles they experienced. She once explained that books

> soothe me and when I have nothing to do I can read a book and I got
> my own library in my room. When I'm upset, I'll read a book. . . .
> The girl in the book, she was angry and she found out a lot of ways
> to make herself happy. Because she would be upset for like 5 minutes
> and go to laughing and talking 'cuz she'll have thoughts and say
> them out loud from reading the books. I was reading her book and
> she was reading a book inside of the book.

One could argue that Paige found solace in books in the same way that conversations with her mother in quiet spaces made Paige feel calm again. Although she could be emotionally fragile after her grandfather passed away, Paige seemed to have learned from her mother and a world of literacy to be more independent and resilient. Perhaps it's not surprising that Paige often read books in which a historical or fictional character struggled and triumphed over some emotional or physical obstacle. For example, when she described studying the Lewis and Clark expedition, she lit up when she spoke about Sacajawea, who served as a guide for about a year. With admiration, Paige reflected on the triumph of a young girl: "She helps translate the languages . . . she was a little girl and remembered some of the trails they went through to help them finish the . . . expedition." At age 12, Paige couldn't help but identify with Sacajawea and imagine her own triumphs. Perhaps this is why she was drawn to autobiographies, "of people and their life and how their life was from when they were as a child growing up. Autobiographies inspired me to write my own. My mom said she is gonna get it published for me so I can have my own book." Writing together, Paige and her mother create an authorial space, a space of hope.

More often than not, Paige expressed an unusual sense of self-confidence that seemed rooted in her parents' belief in her capacity to achieve in school. She also knew that she could rely on them for support and as a source of stability in her life. From our very first conversation it was clear that Paige's mother and father had established an after-school routine for Paige and expected her to complete her homework immediately. She depended on her father for help in math and he often showed her what she described as "neat tricks." She also turned to her mother for help in social studies because, as Paige explained, her mother was always reading and looking up facts that she shared with Paige. In fact, her mother had just acquired a dictionary, which included a lengthy appendix about historical events, famous people, and maps from around the world. Her mother "memorized like a lot of stuff from out of there and she tells me about what happened in 1900s and stuff." According to Paige, they often read together for hours and they often traded stories about what they were learning.

Given her relationship with her parents, it was not surprising that Paige always felt that she could share her tests and graded homework with her parents, even on the rare occasion when she received a low grade. She seemed to understand that if she did get a bad grade, she had to accept it and move on, further evidence of her confidence and developing sense of resilience. Her mother reinforced Paige's attitude when, below, she told Paige to just do better next time and her father simply told her to study more without judging her harshly. They both expressed their support with a great deal of patience and love.

> PAIGE: I showed my parents my papers like I get turned in and all my good grades and my bad grades, too. I only get like one bad grade if something that's new to me and I really got to get used to it.
>
> AUTHOR: If you have a good grade, how do you feel when you show your parents your work?
>
> PAIGE: Happy, excited.
>
> AUTHOR: How do you feel if it's not a good grade?
>
> PAIGE: Not too much excited about it.
>
> AUTHOR: How do your parents usually react?

PAIGE: My momma tell me you can do better next time and my dad, he'll just say, like before we go to bed, he'll say you got to study your math and stuff like that.

Paige's mother also offered a great deal of emotional support. Paige was unnerved by the stress of taking standardized tests and her mother often sat with her before school to reassure her. According to Paige, their conversations "make me feel ready because usually I'll be nervous because my mom, she usually just see if I'm studying, then she'll start helping me when I study and then when I get ready to start the test, I don't be nervous." Paige's mother made many sacrifices to help her, particularly when Paige was in 6th grade and began to lose some of the confidence that she projected in 4th and 5th grade. Her mother left work on more than one occasion to help Paige. At other times, Paige's mother sat beside her to ensure that Paige understood a given assignment.

PAIGE: She'll tell me to come sit down and, uh, she will help me. And sometimes if my mom is cooking dinner or something my dad will help me do it.
AUTHOR: Okay. And when they're helping you, what do they do?
PAIGE: They, um, tell me to get pencil and paper. Sometimes if we need a calculator my dad, he'll use the calculator and help me with equations that I don't know.
AUTHOR: Okay. And then, um, let's see . . . do they ever help you with studying or . . . if you have a test, how do they help with that?
PAIGE: My mom will review questions and answers and then she'll tell me to let her see the paper and go over the questions and see if I memorized the answers.

To further support their daughter when the math in school exceeded their knowledge, Paige's mother and father found a tutor from a local college for her until Paige felt that she understood the work.

Indeed, Paige's parents were proactive in their efforts to create opportunities for Paige and envisioned a future for her that would be different from their own. They did not have access to educational opportunities when they were younger; they struggled economically, especially when Paige's grandfather died; and they had little job security. Paige reflected on her mother's words when, as a 6th-grader, she explained that she wanted to go to college and become a veterinarian. Specifically, her mother advised Paige to "stay in school as long as you can so you won't mess up your life and have to struggle to find out how to make money and get a job." They encouraged her to play sports, sing in the school chorus, and act in the school play; they took her to the historical museum on one occasion where she took notes and then returned to her aunt's house where she could work on the computer and look up "stuff"; and they took her to the local zoo as often as they could to encourage Paige's interest in becoming a veterinarian. More than anything, Paige seemed passionate about her future and was determined to succeed.

ALISKA: "I KNOW THAT I'M A STRONG GIRL"

We learn from Aliska that her parents taught her to value her family and she took on responsibilities that many children her age are never expected to fulfill. Like Paige's parents, Aliska's parents were proactive in their efforts to support their children and challenge a dominant narrative that low-income parents are deferential if not passive (e.g., Lareau, 2003; Rothstein, 2004).

Like Paige, Aliska was 12 years old and in 6th grade at the time I was writing. She lived with her mother, father, and five siblings—three sisters and two brothers—with whom she had a close relationship. Aliska often spoke of family nights when everyone watched a movie together or played Monopoly. And she loved reading to her younger brother. On Saturdays, Aliska routinely spent the afternoon with her family at a newly constructed community center underwritten by a well-known philanthropist and matching grants. The center provided a limited number of youth and their families in the surrounding neighborhood with access to activities that focus on the arts, game rooms, and a fitness center, either at a reduced cost or for free. Aliska also spoke about the symphony she once attended at a performing arts center and the part she just got in a school play, *Seussical the Musical.*

Aliska was a confident girl who explained when she was in 4th grade, "I know that I'm a strong girl. I know that just because somebody says something about me doesn't mean that I'm going to let them ruin my whole day." Some of this self-assurance can be attributed to her relationship with her parents, who taught her a strong work ethic at home and at school where, according to one of her teachers, "She loves to please." She wanted to make sure she's "got the assignment done. She does care about getting good grades. She does care." Aliska discovered on her progress report that there was one assignment that was missing and she kept coming back to her teacher saying that she needed to find the assignment. It was never clear if Aliska failed to turn in the assignment or if the teacher could have misplaced it. Aliska kept asking her teacher what she should do about making up the missed assignment until the teacher finally gave her another assignment to complete.

Aliska acquired a strong sense of responsibility from her parents. She was expected to do her chores when she returned home from school and then immediately finish her homework. On most days, either her mother or father helped her with her work, especially in math. "They'll help me like that, like with my math. This one time, I had a math [problem] and I couldn't get it, and then my dad came in and he drew a picture of it. Then I started getting it more and he was like, there you go you got it. Then I started getting more of it." On another occasion, Aliska explained, "We had this one test and we had some flashcards. I had to work on that and I got that right. I got some part of it right and some part of it wrong, and he was like, not quite, and I was just like, oh wow. And then we did it again and I got them all right." When asked how she felt when she got them all right, she said, "It made me feel happy and confident." Similarly, she wanted to show her parents her schoolwork "Because I put progress in it, and I think it's nice to show somebody about it and see what they think about it."

However, more often than not, Aliska spoke of reading or studying alone because she felt she did not need help. Even in 4th grade, Aliska was growing independent and felt that she should be able to do her work by herself as she got older. She also felt that she always did her best, so that it was fine if she got some answers wrong. In turn, her parents gave her the space she needed by taking what I describe in Chapter 2 as a "hands-off" approach to supporting their daughter. Still, they often monitored Aliska's progress in school by asking her about her schoolwork and by communicating with Aliska's teachers. They knew that she had begun to excel in reading and math, a point Aliska's 6th-grade teacher also observed. However, they grew increasingly concerned with Aliska's ability to control her emotions at school. If Aliska sought to please those around her, she could at times give in to her peers at the cost of challenging her teachers' authority.

Aliska loved school because she felt that she "always learned something new." Indeed, her parents encouraged her to do well in school, and she had developed an intrinsic sense of motivation. She read to herself and chose books that she wanted to read above and beyond the reading her teachers assigned in school. Although she did not see her mother reading much at home—despite the fact that her mother was in school—she explained that her "mom and her mom's mom, my grandma, they're always on us about reading. I'm thinking that [my grandma] was on her kids about reading." Aliska explained that she didn't have favorite books, but really liked mysteries and books that others her age typically read, such as *Katie Kazoo, Judy B. Jones,* and *Frank the Mighty.*

Like Paige, Aliska also loved being surrounded by friends who helped her feel good about herself and who provided an important source of emotional support and acceptance. When she was in 5th grade, she described having lunch in the cafeteria with her friends. "I sit with the girls because I have to, I'm a girl. Everybody sits down where I am at. It's on a table like this. I always sit down here. That's a thing for me, it's my seat down there. Right on the edge. If I sit down there, everybody else goes down there. If I move down here, everybody else goes down there. It's like they're following me or something. I just admire that." But like Paige and other children she knew, Aliska often chafed at her parents' rules about leaving the house. "I can't go far and . . . I tell them where I'm going. I have to call them if I go to the park. I have to ask if I go to the library, I have to, when I get out of school."

By 6th grade, Aliska was reading challenging books, such as *Son of Neptune* and *A Child Called It,* an emotionally troubling book about a boy who is severely abused. She read the books carefully and could recount the details accurately in oral presentations in class, but she resisted completing the written work that her teacher assigned. According to her teacher, she would go up front and "she could tell us everything. Her presentation was beautiful, but there was nothing written on paper." This is surprising because her teacher assured Aliska that her writing skills really were very good. In fact, while Aliska believes that she is better in math, her teacher has told her parents that she is actually stronger in language arts. Unfortunately, Aliska was easily unsettled if she got an assignment where she thought she was going to be graded or timed. She could panic and hardly get anything written down. Thus she needed some encouragement to write.

Aliska enjoyed learning. She wanted to know everything. She was curious. However, Aliska struggled in 6th grade and with tears in her eyes explained that the year had been "kind of rough. This is the worst. This is the only school year that I've ever had this much trouble." Asked to reflect on why she was having "trouble," she was reflective and accepted some responsibility. Referring to her teacher, Aliska explained, "She's trying to keep me, push me because when I get to sixth, seventh, and eighth grade, they're not going to be this easy on me. She's trying to get me used to be how they're going to be when I get in the older grades." It also turned out that Aliska resented the fact that her teacher did not always call on her when she raised her hand, and began to just call out her answers to her teacher's questions. As Compton-Lilly (2007) suggests, children often have a strong sense of fairness, turn-taking, and acceptable behavior based on their interactions with friends and family members. In this case, Aliska felt threatened when she believed her teacher failed to recognize her fought-for sense of individuality, whereas her teacher may have simply wanted to encourage other students to speak up in class.

Aliska recounted the conversation she had with her parents and brought to the fore some of the emotional problems she was facing, both in and out of class.

> ALISKA: We're talking about when I got in trouble yesterday. About my write-up that I had yesterday.
> AUTHOR: What happened with that?
> ALISKA: We were talking about what happened. She was like, "When I see you talking again, then I'm writing you up." I was like, "Okay." Then I went to go get my pencil and go sharpen it and she wrote me up and said that I was being disruptive to the class, wasn't following directions, insubordinate and being disrespectful, and every time I'm getting on my seat . . . every time she writes me up, she's saying I'm being insubordinate.
> AUTHOR: You told your family all of that?
> ALISKA: Mm-hmm. (*Affirmative*)
> AUTHOR: How did they react?
> ALISKA: They said that they were going to call or go into the school because I've been having problems with her, too. That's the only teacher I've been having problems with. They said they were either going to call or go into the school and see if I can either get a transfer to other classes or transfer to a different school.

It's important that Aliska's parents were willing and able to have critical conversations like this one with their daughter. In turn, they also spent a great deal of time with Aliska's teacher. Her mother, in particular, had forged a consistent relationship with the teacher and Aliska began to see that they were talking. In turn, her mother was able to help her see that her teacher might have been tough on Aliska, but that her teacher also cared. It also mattered that the teacher's conversations with Aliska's mother gave the teacher a window into Aliska's specific needs. That is, although the teacher appreciated Aliska's abilities as a student, she also recognized the importance of helping Aliska by explaining the purpose behind her actions in class—that she was holding Aliska to a high standard academically but also teaching her to respect both her own authority as a teacher and the needs of other students.

In the end, Aliska's parents held their daughter to a high standard and talked with Aliska about school, going to college, and the emotional challenges that at times made it difficult for Aliska to do her best work in school. Aliska's teacher attributed Aliska's developing self-awareness to communicating with her parents and other significant adults in Aliska's life. Indeed, they were well aware that Aliska wanted to be a teacher of English and supported her. Aliska had come to this decision, at least for the time being, after watching the news with her family. They watched the news together often and their conversations provided a context for talking about Aliska's future. On this occasion, she said that she was struck by the number of people in China whom she believed didn't know English.

> ALISKA: I saw on the news that a lot of people in China don't understand what Americans are saying so like, I can bring people there and they can transfer the language to them.
> AUTHOR: Does your family know that you want to be a Chinese teacher?
> ALISKA: Mm-hmm.
> AUTHOR: Did they ask you or did you tell them?
> ALISKA: I told them.
> AUTHOR: And what did they say?
> ALISKA: They said, wow that's good.
> AUTHOR: And how did they make you feel about wanting to be a Chinese teacher?
> ALISKA: They made me feel good.

Not only did Aliska's parents set up the expectation that they wanted Aliska to attend college, but they supported her by fostering her self-confidence and sense of agency. This was evident when Aliska explained that they encouraged her to do well in school and that they were already saving for college.

Although Aliska's plans could change, her conversations about education with her family extended beyond the classroom into the arena of world events, and she began to imagine a world beyond her own neighborhood where she might have a place to teach. With her parents' support, she had also begun to develop a sense of civic responsibility and to see the value of reaching out to others in need, again in the context of world events. Aliska and her parents had been discussing the earthquake in Haiti and ways that they could be of help. Rarely did they place limits on what Aliska thought she could do in creating a world of possibilities.

JASMINE: "THERE ARE TWO ROADS. I GO TO THE RIGHT ROAD"

Jasmine's story sheds light on the value that peers can have in motivating children to learn and the fact that parents' involvement may manifest itself both directly and indirectly. But parents' efforts and the presence of friends and family move in and out of the foreground depending on what children need over time. By all accounts, Jasmine was drawn to friends who shared a similar ethic of success and achievement, and her parents helped her navigate opportunities and risk at school by teaching her to maintain a clear focus on her education.

Jasmine's parents instilled in their daughter from an early age a clear sense that she could accomplish anything, and they were a constant presence in her life. In 4th grade, when she first spoke about wanting to be a teacher, she explained that her parents always supported her: "They tell me you can be whatever you want to be and they just let me follow my dreams and get good scholarships and like do good things." In 5th grade, Jasmine reiterated her goal of becoming a teacher and a basketball player, inspired by a very charismatic young woman who graduated from a local high school and who had gained national prominence. Asked again if her parents supported her goals, she said they told her, "Do the right thing always and if somebody is like trying to be mean to me or something, just put your hand down and just leave them to do something else." At the end of 6th grade, Jasmine echoed her earlier reflections about her future and perhaps a maturity beyond her years: "They let me follow my dream. They just lead me to the right path and not the wrong one, like there's two roads, I go to the right road."

Jasmine's mother had worked at the primary school Jasmine attended, met her after school, and helped her with her homework. I had first spoken to Jasmine when she was in the 4th grade, and I asked her who helped her study. She immediately said, "My mom. She's been helping me since second grade. We get into our dining room and just talk and then do my homework together." She sees her mother reading all of the time, and yet Jasmine has said, "I am a math girl." Indeed, she loved math and often spoke of sitting with her mother to solve math problems in 5th grade when math was getting harder for her.

> She helps me every time we have a test like, teacher, she warned us about like studying and stuff. So when I go home, I tell her read the questions to me. We had this, these problems like median mode and this other thing, and then um, I didn't understand what mode meant. I kept asking her and asking her and she helped me, like 'cause she went to the page in um, modes on and then she helped me understand what mode means. 'Cause I really didn't know what that means, and that's it.

Jasmine mentioned that studying with her mother always felt "good because I know that I can do it and I feel confident." She also felt compelled to share all of her schoolwork with her parents because they made it clear that they wanted to know how she was doing. Moreover, they did not want any "surprises" when they met with Jasmine's teachers.

Jasmine explained that "if we have a parent/teacher conference or something and then they come up to the school, my mom is like, 'She didn't show me that' and then I'd just get in trouble."

Jasmine's parents taught her other life lessons as well. Like Aliska, Jasmine was expected to do her chores around the house after she completed her homework. By the time she was in 6th grade she also began to take more responsibility for her three younger siblings. Jasmine helped them with breakfast before she left for school and read to them every day. "Yeah. I read to my two little sisters. 'Cause my brother, he's not in school yet. So I read to my two little sisters. And I signed a paper and told the stories about what kind of book they read."

Recognizing her potential and love of math, Jasmine's parents enrolled her in a 1-day program called Girl Power at a local woman's college. The aim of the program was to mentor young girls, foster their interest in math and science, and help them see that math and science were legitimate fields of study for women. This was just one example of the ways in which Jasmine's parents not only supported their daughter, but advocated for her by opening up opportunities and helping to build both her self-esteem and resilience, so she could flourish in the sense that Grant (2012) has used the term. They instilled in her the understanding that she should just "leave them [others who are mean or discourage her] to do something else" and just follow the "right road." They helped her develop a sense of well-being and the critical capacity to make good decisions about her life's path.

Lareau (2003) has characterized low-income families as adopting a "natural growth model" in the ways that they raise their children. The parents of all three girls challenge such a model in the ways in which they structure their children's lives around opportunities for after-school tutoring, trips to the zoo to encourage their interests, participating in plays, or spending the afternoon at a community center. Indeed, Jasmine was on the basketball team in 6th grade; had a lead in the play *Seussical the Musical*, the same play that Paige had a role in; practiced singing with her father, who had a modest recording studio at home; and spent a great deal of time at church, where she was learning about character formation. Like the other children in the area, she rarely spent time outside in her neighborhood because she recognized that "things can get dangerous." In 6th grade, she reflected on her father's role in her life.

JASMINE: It's mostly my dad. He will say, "How was school today?" Then, we just talk about how school was.

AUTHOR: Can you remember a conversation you had with them, the last time you talked to them?

JASMINE: I talked to my dad yesterday. I'm having a ceremony at the . . . I have to go to this thing called Daughters of Destiny at the church.

AUTHOR: What is that?

JASMINE: It's called Daughters of Destiny and then it's at church. We learn about good character, God is watching us always and all of that stuff. I'm having a ceremony on Saturday.

Not unlike many of the families and children whose stories fill the pages of *Race, Community, and Urban Schools*, faith is a central part of Jasmine's life. Jasmine connected with her 6th-grade math teacher not only because Jasmine loved math, but also because religion served as a common ground between them. Jasmine and her parents saw Jasmine's teacher every Sunday at church. In turn, Jasmine sought to please her teacher and felt comfortable "telling her everything."

Jasmine's parents also forged a relationship with her teachers as one of the unfortunate consequences of a fire that forced Jasmine's family from their home. Even this near-tragic circumstance provided Jasmine with a lesson in resilience and self-reliance. Her mom told her, "It doesn't matter what happened at home, keep your grades up." They were living with a friend when Jasmine completed 6th grade, but she never missed an assignment and maintained her high grades.

MINELIK: "READING IS KIND OF LIKE THE TV BUT ALL PUT INTO A BOOK"

Thus far, children's stories indicate the extent to which relationships matter in children's growth, development, and personal well-being. Although Minelik's parents provided a sense of stability and modeled what they expected of him, Minelik was a quiet child whose network of support was limited to his family and a few friends. This limited network set him apart from Paige, Aliska, and Jasmine, and perhaps made him more vulnerable, both emotionally and academically, in his life as a student.

A solitary child, Minelik saw himself as a "good" student who worked hard in 4th grade. In his words, he "listened to the teacher . . . did not talk out loud, and didn't horse around at the wrong time." He was attentive and learned to do what his parents and teachers expected of him. Compliant, Minelik adopted the identity of a well-behaved student who did not want to call attention to himself. He wanted to excel and completed his schoolwork as soon as he returned home from school each day. At the time we spoke, when he was in 4th grade, he explained that he knew he was a good student because "my behavior's good and I know, like a whole bunch of stuff."

Even as a 4th-grader, Minelik described himself as fairly independent yet proactive, rarely asking his parents for help studying or reading. His routine each day entailed coming home from school, reading quietly, and doing his homework before he got on the computer to "play the game" or meet a few friends nearby to play basketball—his true passion. Still, his parents were very much a presence for Minelik and both monitored and encouraged his academic progress. One of his earliest recollections focused on how often his mother read to him in 1st grade. His mother, in particular, often asked him what he was reading and stressed the value of reading as way to learn. In addition to providing encouragement, she also served as an important role model whom Minelik described as an active reader. She was always reading the Bible and he connected with his mother by sitting and reading with her. This intimacy between mother and son mirrors the image of Paige reading with her mother at the edge of her bed.

Minelik was confident and enjoyed school because he felt he was learning new things. This sense of confidence fueled some of his independence as a 4th-grader, but he still showed his parents all of his work. He wanted to share what he was doing in school, and if he was unsure about something, Minelik sought his parents' help.

By the time he was in 6th grade, Minelik's schoolwork was becoming more difficult and demanding. Minelik also felt more pressure in school because teachers were devoting more time to preparing students for standardized tests. Minelik's observations reflected the sense of urgency at his school, which had not achieved Annual Yearly Progress in 4 years. Thus, the state superintendent of public instruction had placed the school on probation. As a response to this decision to place the school on probation, the local school corporation replaced the principal at Minelik's school with the expectation that the new principal would help raise test scores.

Minelik's parents were helping him more because they recognized that he had begun to struggle in school. He explained, "Every week we have a Language Arts test on words that we need to know for I-STEP and our reading. It's very hard words that you have to study for. You have a test and my mom studies with me at home. She tells me the definition and I have to know the word." Minelik's mother quizzed him on his vocabulary and spelling words each day. His mother did what she could to support her son's development as a reader, and home literacy began to mirror school with daily quizzes. She also worked at his side so that he could complete a project that required him to make an oral presentation in class, something he had never done before. In this case, he was working on a book report about *Hotel for Dogs*:

> Minelik: It's a book report that we got to do, and we got to get a big sheet of poster paper and stuff. We had to write out a character and describe a conflict and the setting. What happened in the story and stuff. My mom helped me with it because it was pretty hard.
>
> Author: What did she do to help you?
>
> Minelik: She asked me questions like the teacher would ask, like, "What did you read about and stuff," and then I tell her, then I write it down.

She took a similar approach to helping Minelik with math. "Like if I don't get it, then she'll like, she'll just write an example on the paper." His father also helped. "He'll work the problem out first, get the answer, and then show me how to do it so I'll get it."

Minelik's mother continued to encourage him to read, and he liked reading to his younger cousin in the same way that his mother read to him when Minelik was in 1st grade. Proud of the collection of books he had in his room, Minelik read books such as *Junie B. Jones*, *Diary of a Wimpy Kid*, and sometimes cartoon books for pure enjoyment, not for school. Minelik once said he enjoyed reading because of the images that words helped create for him. "It's kind of like the TV but all put into a book." It's quite possible that the positive image of his mother reading alone all of the time reinforced Minelik's understanding that reading is a solitary activity. Thus, he explained on several occasions that he preferred reading by himself.

> Minelik: Like when my mom's home, if I need to read, then I'll read alone.
>
> Author: Mm-hmm.
>
> Minelik: She said like if I need to get my reading level up, then I'll just go in there like I read like twice a day, like two chapters a day.

In 6th grade, Minelik attended a special class each day to practice on and improve his reading comprehension. The class was led by a reading teacher who asked students to answer questions about character, setting, and plot in the books they were reading. These classes were structured and scripted in ways that reflected the emphasis placed on a limited number of skills in standardized tests of reading comprehension. Thus, it is not surprising that when asked what a good reader is in 6th grade, Minelik said, "Someone who does not read too fast, but not too slow . . . [who] understands and gives you facts." Indeed, he had become socialized to think of reading as a set of behaviors and that the aim of reading was to answer questions on a worksheet or to pass a quiz. This was a far cry from the intimacy that reading with his mother provided or the conversations they shared when he was younger. Still, Minelik enjoyed reading for reasons that belie his definition of reading. He still liked to slip away to his room "with the door closed so it will be silent" and where he could enjoy the images that books evoked for him. He especially liked one book that didn't have any words, "so you have to predict the stuff with your mind." In this way, he could "come up with [his] own stories." He also liked *Chillers* and other books that fit into the category of horror, but he also was drawn to books such as *Hip-Hop High School* and *Homeboyz*, each of which focus on themes of gang activity and violence in deteriorating neighborhoods like his own.

Missing for Minelik was the sense of support at school that Paige described or the places in the community that nurtured Jasmine. Clearly, Minelik's family was a strong, important influence on him; he enjoyed the closeness that he had developed with his parents and looked forward to family nights when he played games or watched a movie. However, it was also telling that, in 6th grade, Minelik looked forward to spending time with his family as opposed to having to work on projects such as the book report he did on *Hotel for Dogs*.

> AUTHOR: How do you feel when you spend time with your family?
> MINELIK: Good.
> AUTHOR: Good? Can you explain that a little more?
> MINELIK: Right. It's better than being in that school.
> AUTHOR: Mm-hmm. *(Affirmative)*
> MINELIK: You get to have fun with them instead of doing projects and stuff.

Minelik's parents became concerned when he began to struggle in 6th grade because math and reading no longer seemed to come easily to him. Special classes, worksheets, and projects made school less fun for him.

Minelik's parents were also concerned that their 16-year-old son had lost interest in school and they no longer felt that they could control his actions. In Minelik's words, "He isn't doing what my parents say sometimes." Consequently, they felt a sense of urgency to ensure that Minelik understood the value of education and the importance of going to college. In fact, Minelik's parents consistently spoke to him about his future, even though the image of the future they held out was less clear than it was for

Paige, Aliska, or Jasmine. Minelik reported his parents' guidance as follows: "'There's a lot of things out there.' My mom said, 'You don't got to pick right now because you're young.'"

CHILDREN'S STORIES AS COUNTERNARRATIVES

Parents structured their children's lives with the tools they had to ensure that their children flourished. They did their best to draw upon a wellspring of resources and stories to foster their children's resilience, empathy, independence, social responsibility, motivation, and high aspirations. Indeed, children's stories offer a counternarrative to deficit perspectives of low-income families of color by describing the cultural wealth they acquired from their parents. Their stories provided a window through which to understand how what students learned at home and in the community can be viewed as a "cultural knowledge base" that helps students negotiate the challenges they face in school and in the identities that they are beginning to fashion for themselves. Their families served as sources of "inspiration and motivation to overcome obstacles" in formal schooling (Delgado Bernal, 2002), and we learn what matters most to children.

Children's stories allow us to better understand the assets and different types of knowledge that children carry with them from home. Their stories challenge key assumptions:

- Scholars have argued that low-income minority students come from impoverished families who do not support or value literacy at home, yet children's stories reveal the extent to which their homes are filled with print and literacy is an integral part of their lives.
- Children help us see that literacy practices are complex and collaborative. The transmission of literacy is not simply from parent to child. That is, the extent to which parents were involved and the role that they constructed for themselves often depended on what their children needed at the time (Grolnick & Slowiaczek, 1994), which emphasizes the role that children play in motivating parent involvement.
- There is not a simple correlation among parents' backgrounds, levels of education, and time spent with children on literacy activities and achievement.
- Parents may not always have access to economic, political, and social capital, but parents find ways to support their children and help them flourish.

Children's stories tell us that parents are doing a great deal to create opportunities for their children in the face of any number of risk factors that affect these families daily. Parents provided children with what they needed indirectly and directly, whether it was by instilling the value of reading and education or helping them develop a sense of resilience, belonging, responsibility, family, faith, and community.

Listening to children's stories helped me appreciate how families supported their children's learning and growth, even when their parents may have had limited time, material resources, and skills to guide them. Parents are active in seeking the cultural resources that are available and affordable to them, especially libraries, museums, and zoos, but not all parents could take advantage of some opportunities as frequently as they would have liked. In fact, limits on time prevented some of them from waiting on lines to sign up their children for programs even when they were aware of a given program at the library, the school, or a local community center. Months might have passed between visits to the library and a year for visits to a zoo or a museum. Moreover, the tools, skills, and sources of information available to the children at school were not necessarily available at home. Still, children's narratives make visible the level of parents' support and the extent to which children's struggles in school may not be attributed to a lack of parent involvement. As others have observed, the social isolation that children experienced may very well affect their growth and development more than family structure (e.g., Lawrence-Lightfoot, 2003).

In a broad sense, differences in access to educational resources underscore a social justice issue—namely, the unequal distribution of capital (Berliner, 2014; Rothstein, 2004), which explains differences in achievement at a structural level rather than any inherent deficit in children and families. Bourdieu's construct of capital (1993) is relevant here. A key assumption is that inequalities limit the amounts of capital that individuals have or are able to obtain. One source of inequality is economic capital, which enables some families to acquire books, computers, and educational toys that can help children succeed, and which also gives them access to costly reading programs (Compton-Lilly, 2007). A second source is what Bourdieu refers to as social capital—that is, the relationships that parents have access to in order to support their children's education. These relationships can be among family members, friends, school personnel, and experts on whom parents can rely to gain advantage for children. Social capital can provide a resource for knowing what programs in reading exist and how to enroll children in these programs.

Compton-Lilly (2007) underscores a third source—cultural capital—which manifests itself in three ways: personal dispositions, attitudes, and knowledge gained from experience (e.g., mannerisms and the ways that people learn to comport themselves within different contexts); familiarity with education-related materials and practices (e.g., reading the "right" books); and familiarity with educational institutions (e.g., different social practices, procedures, and rules, including increased standards, testing, and accountability). The greater a given family's cultural capital, the more advantage that family has to the resources their children need to flourish. The less capital, the more constraints, resulting in less access to institutional resources.

By observing parents working with children at home in a school-like fashion—grading just like school, writing down examples—I wonder if the home environment is becoming too much like the formal school environment, where the pressures of standards, testing, and accountability exert themselves in children's and teachers' everyday lives. It may simply be unwise to take a narrow view of how parents should contribute to their children's education in ways that support the status quo by focusing on achievement rather than doing what's in children's best interests by focusing on learning. As educators, we can encourage parents to foster their children's "creativity, psychological health, and excitement about learning" (Kohn, 2013).

As I suggest in this chapter, it's important to consider the role that children want their parents to play. Teachers and parents alike would benefit from knowing how excited children became when they described the projects they worked on and the books that touched their lives. Learning follows different paths, and children's stories help us to see the value of reading for different purposes: to form relationships, to imagine "stuff," to broaden their social worlds, to fashion a literate identity, and to write in ways that can be empowering. It matters that children are reading, and more reading correlates with learning that may or may not be measurable. It also matters that children see the value of learning for its own sake at home and at school. As one teacher has put it, "We cannot enrich the minds of our students by testing" (Hollander, 2012). Instead, children need more time in creative, supportive, and safe spaces where they know they are valued, where they can develop meaningful relationships with other children, and where they can flourish by connecting what they learn in school to their day-to-day lives.

The chorus of voices of children with which I began this chapter brings to mind the intimacy of families going to the library and studying together and, as one child put it so poignantly, "We're spending time together and he's helping me, and that just feels good because some people don't have parents that are there to help them." Families instill in children a belief in themselves, a sense that they have a future. For example, "My mother told me that when I grow up and get my education I [can] set [my] mind on being whatever [I] want to be." It is equally important to recognize the myriad of experiences that shape who children are and what they value, and the intersections of race, class, gender, and culture that complicate the identities of children and their families. Literacy instruction, for example, can draw on parents' strengths and encourage critical thinking about key issues in family life. That is, parents' cultural knowledge serves as a resource that contributes to rather than conflicts with school learning. Parents can also address issues emerging at school in the context of their children's experiences. The stories in this chapter should prompt educators to think about ways to serve increasingly diverse children whose needs change over time and do not follow a linear developmental path. Gadsden (1996) argued, "Work with family literacy must unravel assumptions and encourage strong learning contexts respectful of the lived experiences and goals of parents, children, and other family learners" (p. 34).

As in the case of the parents' stories in Chapter 2, the children's narratives prompt me to think about the need for neighborhood schools and public spaces. Unfortunately, parents' stories also show us the extent to which economic and school policy conspire to undermine community connections and the social capital that children and families work so hard to create. Similarly, the children's narratives should prompt us all "to reign in the all-consuming culture of assessment and move toward education that is humane and relational, not based solely on individual markers of success and failure." Perhaps our greatest challenge in our efforts to cultivate children's flourishing lives is to find ways to "integrate and cultivate schools and communities as mutually supportive spheres in youth's lives. If schools and communities are to play such a role, then it follows that building relationships should be a central focus" (Greene, Burke, & McKenna, 2013, p. 332).

CONCLUSION

I end this chapter by again calling attention to the Adult-Child Imaginary and the value of letting children author their own stories at the intersections of race, class, gender, and culture that complicate the identities of children and their families. As ethnographers of children, we can interpret what children need based on increased knowledge of who children and families are, what they value, and the challenges they experience at home, at school, and in the community. Children must learn to navigate each of these spaces, and their stories reveal a great deal about their capacities and the challenges they face within a broad sociocultural and economic landscape. Therefore, Lawrence-Lightfoot (2003) has argued that teachers who are working with parents must do everything in their power to put children—their strengths and their vulnerabilities, their achievements, and their challenges—at the center of their relationships with parents.

In the next chapter, I focus on parents' sense of urgency to support their children's education in the face of their own unrealized dreams and an economic climate that conspires against parents' efforts to reverse a cycle of relative poverty. To replace all-too-common deficit perspectives, I provide a model of communicating that emphasizes reciprocity, listening, and empathy to foster partnerships between parents and teachers that are necessary if, as educators, we expect children to flourish.

CHAPTER 4

Schools as Inclusive and Exclusionary Spaces

We all have a lot of similarities from childhood, a lot of mistakes that were made per se with us. What we talk about mostly is breaking the cycle. Somebody, somewhere has to break the cycle, get things back on track and get the kids the way that it should be. I believe that kids need discipline, love, and consistency.

—Amy, parent at Ida B. Wells

It's just I'm really concerned about his education. This is the first time he's been put into a class where they're reading a lot. I had to push for a test because I knew he had a learning disability. So I hope he can get something, because I think I miss a lot of stuff, especially with the writing. I go to the diversity program at the library and I get a tutor once a week and he helps with my writing.

—Carol, parent at Ida B. Wells

They're coming to you because they have a history and you can't change that history overnight. But, at the most, maybe you could make a connection. And, I think it's very, very slight how you can see, you know, the effects that it has.

—A teacher at Ida B. Wells

Amy lived with her mother until she was 13, when for the next 4 years she entered a number of orphanages, group homes, and foster homes. Amy was alone by the time she was 17, when her mother was raped and the subsequent trauma seemed to swallow up her mother's life, leaving her unable to care for Amy. Although Amy completed high school, she admits that it was a struggle because she was pregnant: "I was working at night trying to maintain my apartment, take care of my child, and finish school but I did it so, I mean, some days I came and I was there in body but that was about it." When she reflects on this period of her life she does so with a sense of triumph in her voice.

Now a single mom after getting herself out of what she called "a physically abusive relationship," Amy has seven children. An avid reader, Amy lives 2 miles from Ida B. Wells in what she describes as a "close-knit" neighborhood with a number of other single mothers who are "always looking out for each other's kids." Together, they are trying to find a way to "break the cycle." One way to accomplish this, she believes, is to provide kids with "discipline, love, and consistency." As we also learn in Chapter 2, Amy has taught her children the value of family, resilience, and persistence in the face of the economic struggles they have experienced. As she puts it, "We need to struggle together [rather] than everybody trying to pull their separate ways, you know." She teaches her children important lessons of surviving together as a family and that they will indeed come out on the other side.

Carol, another parent of an Ida B. Wells student, describes herself as "pretty much the Black girl in a White neighborhood" when she was in school. She now lives in a more mixed neighborhood, a 20-minute drive from the school. Carol graduated from high school and received an accounting degree from a small religiously oriented college located in the city where she lives. She was drawn to math because she had a learning disability, which made it difficult for her to read and write: "I struggled with writing. I didn't like doing reports." She had started at another college, but had to leave because, in her words, she "never really studied." After she changed colleges and moved closer to home, she worked with a tutor and did quite well. She now works for the state and has four children, one of whom has a learning disability and struggles in school. As an advocate for her son, Carol explains that she has had to "push" for a test to certify his learning disability, which would enable him to receive extra support from the school district. After all, she wants to ensure that the school provides sufficient support now that "he's been put into a class where they're reading a lot." She does not want him to struggle the way she did. In fact, she has sought out a tutor to help her with her own writing to enable her to support her son's developing literacy skills.

As I've argued in Chapter 2, these parents are active supporters of their children's education in a number of ways. Less visible to many of us is the legacy of schooling that has influenced the ways that parents view educators and an institution that has failed them and, for many, their children. This is a point that one teacher at Ida B. Wells made in addressing parent involvement: "They're coming to you because they have a history and you can't change that history overnight." Like their children, parents of color "arrive at schools with complex narratives of purposes, possibilities, and disappointments of schooling" (Auerbach, 2001 p. 1369). As Auerbach explains, parents view the educational process—and their own agency—through the lens of their own experiences. The way that parents perceive school "mediates their understandings and actions around schooling" (2001, p. 1369; see also Rogers, 2003). Parents' experiences help us to see that at times teachers can be inattentive to students' needs as learners and that parents can feel as if they are invisible with really no voice in the decisions that teachers make about their children's needs. Parents' stories in Chapter 2 tell us that parents see the disconnect between the pace of instruction and their children's struggle to understand new information; between the assignments their children's teachers send home and the lack of instruction to guide their children's efforts to complete their homework; and the grades that their children receive in class and their scores on standardized tests.

Shifting parents' positioning on the landscape of schools from the margins to the center entails making sure that schools serve parents' purposes. Therefore, it is important to ask what it would mean for teachers, parents, and children to interact with one another in ways that would be consistent with a democracy and that would give legitimacy to different types of knowledge. Specifically, how can we engage parents in the core work of schooling? Addressing this question can allow us to reimagine places where parents and teachers both tell their own histories and challenge the dominant narratives that perpetuate inequality. Such a question also underscores the need to develop "culturally appropriate definitions and family-centered practices" (Auerbach, 2007, p. 253) that challenge traditional models, which ignore "non-traditional" practices of engagement.

Equally important, parents' legacies of schooling (and those of their own parents) call attention to long-standing disparities in urban public schools, grossly inequitable allocation of resources, racial segregation, and the failure of public policy to address poverty and racial inequality after decades of disinvestment in physical, economic, and social infrastructure in neighborhoods where African Americans and other people of color live (Anyon, 2005). These disparities find their sources in shifts in the political economy that emphasize free markets, individual responsibility, and choice. Invoking a history of Black activism, Tillman (2004) has observed that educators cannot afford to ignore the lack of public trust and commitment to schools. School systems have been complicit in reproducing inequality, and have long failed to educate students of color by adhering to models of teaching and learning that treat difference as a deficit.

As I mention in Chapter 1, I worry that teachers can too easily attribute children's struggles in school to parents' deficits in knowledge and their failure to "do their job," as one teacher at Ida B. Wells put it.

Similarly, another teacher ascribed her students' struggles to a deficit in parents' levels of literacy: "I don't think my parents can read or I don't think my parents can write." In addition, she challenges parents' ability to parent because, in her mind, they don't know how to "bring their children along." If parents do not possess the knowledge, skills, and resources that this teacher identifies as needed, then she seems to suggest that she cannot be an effective teacher. After all, children will not know "sight words" or "comprehend" what they read in class. For this teacher and others at Ida B. Wells, parents can best support teachers by creating consistency between home and school. It seems to follow that if children do not grasp basic concepts in class, then parents must not be fulfilling their responsibilities.

Of course, it is reasonable to expect parents to create a space where children can do their work, ensure that their children complete their homework, talk with them about their interests, and expose their children to varied experiences outside of school. As I have suggested in *Race, Community, and Urban Schools*, many parents are doing these things, even though teachers may not readily see increases in children's understanding of concepts and test scores. "Parents are in a different place," one teacher observed, but she also insisted that parents and teachers want "the same things." The challenge is how parents or teachers are able to cross boundaries, gain mutual understanding, and become partners in children's education. It is equally important to see that parents' involvement may have different effects for some children more than others and may not be the most important factor in student success in the classroom (Lee & Bowen, 2006).

If parents and teachers are indeed in different places, then one way to cross boundaries is to understand who parents are and what they most want for their children. Moreover, a more reciprocal conception of parent involvement would place dialogue at the center of any relationship between teachers and parents as a means for understanding the extent to which teachers and parents actually "share the same [goals]." Parents and teachers occupy different social positions, and the unequal relations of power that define the relationships between teachers and parents can easily mute parents' voices in deciding what is best for their children. This is significant because the decisions that educators make can determine the life paths of children.

Conversation is a means for working toward developing shared understanding and empathy (Greene, 2001)—that is, the ability to understand another person's worldview, to identify with such a perspective, and to grasp the reasons why people adopt particular ways of seeing the world in the ways that they do. Seen in this way, conversation involves both listening to what people say with respect and trying to understand the underlying reasons for their silences. If we allow ourselves to listen in these ways, it is possible to experience what one scholar describes as "a sympathetic passing over into the other's life and stories" (Fasching, cited in Marty, 2005, p. 132).

Reciprocity can serve as a means for parents and teachers to cross boundaries and begin to level the playing field on which the very notion of parent involvement exists. By reciprocity, I mean the ways that people balance their needs and expectations with what they believe others need. Reciprocity is critical to effective home-school relationships, since conversation is, by definition, a two-way flow of information. In Chapter 2, I quoted one administrator at Ida B. Wells, whose words underscore the potential of conversation as a tool for enhancing mutual understanding and cooperation. He also affirms the value of listening to parents and what they need to help their children flourish:

> Communication should foster a cooperative relationship between the two stakeholders, you know, in the process of saying let us work together and, you know, what would you like to see happen, what would you like to have available for your child? What things can we do together and work on together?

Parents need to know what is going on in school (e.g., classroom events, field trips, curriculum) and teachers need to know about a family's needs, interests, histories, and events.

A key part of fostering a truly reciprocal understanding between parents and teachers relates to parents' own educational experiences and histories, which have such a profound influence on parents' goals for their children. Schools exist in time and space, and they embed memories that give meaning to those spaces. Parents recall the warmth of relationships, laughter, successes, and hopes and dreams; they also have memories of alienation, of teachers who did not seem to care about their future, and teachers who eroded both their self-esteem and their sense of belonging. Writing about the challenges of crossing boundaries for teachers and parents, Lawrence-Lightfoot (2003) underscores the extent to which parents' childhood narratives get "recast and replayed" as parents attempt to advocate for their children and both parents and teachers come together "haunted by the ghosts of their early family and school experiences" (p. 109). Thus, conversations are shaped by "autobiographical stories and by the broader cultural and historical narratives that inform their identities, their values, and their sense of place in the world" (p. 4). To use the metaphor of space and critical geography, the terrain between families and schools is defined by boundary lines that may be either psychological or literal, when, for example, parents enter a classroom to meet their children's teachers.

In the remainder of this chapter, we hear parents' stories about growing up in low-income, segregated neighborhoods, and parents teach us about the resilience and independence they developed both in school and outside of school that they now impart to their children. We also learn that parents' experiences as adults serve as a source for motivating their children to succeed in school, whether or not these experiences were positive or negative. They identify their children's education as a priority. However, teachers rarely have the opportunity to hear parents' stories outside of a traditional parent-teacher conference, and may not know how to develop the kind of conversation that can create a trusting, collaborative relationship. Further, teachers may not always realize the importance of parents' backgrounds as a way to forge relationships that can help children excel in school. I end this chapter by concluding that the challenge of crossing borders for parents and teachers is a structural problem that can only be addressed in a climate of reciprocity, dialogue, empathy, and a mutual respect for differences.

PARENTS' LEGACIES OF SCHOOLING

Parents' biographies provide insight into their own experiences in school; the value they place on their children's education, particularly the purposes that literacy and learning serve; and the roles they construct for themselves. Although the parents at Ida B. Wells had widely divergent memories of their own education and their levels of academic achievement varied, they uniformly identified their children's education as a priority. They believed that education is the key to their children's future. For example, Maya, whose troubled and violent past kept her from pursuing her education past middle school, explained, "I try to tell my kids that you need your education 'cause [otherwise] you will be lost." Similarly, Lamont, who could not read despite having completed high school, stated with some urgency, "You know, that's the main thing, you have to stick with school, you know, 'cause that's your life. You don't have to know everything, but you have to know something to stay alive in this world, you know." It is telling that Lamont retained his faith in schools despite the extent to which his teachers failed him. Having dropped out in middle school, Therese wanted her six children "to be better and more successful because it's just, everything is just changing. You know, my kids have to have an education." As I indicate in Chapter 2, Marc strove to motivate his sons by serving as a role model in the community by mentoring youth and helping at the homeless center. After all, he said, "You always want your children to do a little bit better than you've done." He was well aware of his own lost opportunities in school. Like Amy, who gave voice to her struggles at the beginning of this chapter, the parents I worked with at Ida B. Wells shared her sense that they needed to "break the cycle."

Richard's story, which I began to relate in Chapter 2, is worth telling in some detail because it serves as a contrast to the challenging and even negative school experiences that other parents have narrated. Still, these two very different types of experiences both result in a similar focus on school and a commitment to education as a means of success. Richard's parents completed high school, and although he himself did not complete high school, he eventually received his GED. He liked school and recalled with pride that he made it to the finals in the state spelling bee in 6th grade. His teacher provided a great deal of help, and his most memorable experiences center on primary school, where he believes his teachers really cared about him: "I felt like I was wanted, you know, every kid needs to have a teacher that care about 'em and that wants them to learn, and if you got a teacher that is just teaching 'em and not caring about what's going on in their life it's not gonna help that kid learn anything." Richard's sense of care motivates him to advocate for his son, particularly if he believes that a teacher does not follow through on a promise to contact him about his son's progress. This was the case when Richard asked his son's teacher to let him know if his son was missing any assignments. Not until Richard saw his son's report card did he realize that the teacher failed to let him know that his son was falling behind.

Richard had little support from his parents when he was growing up. After all, his father worked two jobs and his mother was a nurse: "She worked all day long, you know, so it was kinda hectic." However, Richard went on to explain that his father did read the Bible to his children on weekends and asked his children to write what they learned. He explained, "My dad would read the Bible to us and then he would start asking us what we learned during the week, and would have us write it on a piece of paper. What we learned was like a book report. And he would read it and stuff like that."

By the time he was in high school, Richard felt that the teachers did not have the same kind of interest in their students that his teachers in elementary school did.

> It seemed like some of the teachers didn't care about us learning too much, it was more like get the work done and come back to school . . . They didn't pay more attention to the kids, you know certain kids need more help than others, they felt like if one knows it all the

rest should know it, and it's not like that . . . so I really didn't feel comfortable in school, so I had a kid at sixteen and that's when I dropped out.

In making this observation, Richard echoes other parents who are concerned that instruction often outpaces children's development and level of education.

Ayesha, another Ida B. Wells parent with mixed school experiences, describes herself as "quiet," someone who "loved" to learn: "I would watch the kids outside playing and stuff. I'd be in the house reading a book, or playing school or something." Ayesha had always loved to read, and her mother often worked with her on math and spelling before the family fractured after her parents' divorce. Her mother provided support, high expectations, and love.

> Like we was working on our time tables, she would have us to write 'em, then we had to memorize 'em. She would have us write our sentences and picking out what each of 'em were, what each of the words were. She would sit us down at the table and we would have to spend at least a couple hours every day studying, doing some type of work whether it was homework or whether it was studying.

However, she explained that school was difficult and she dropped out before she ever made it to high school. Unfortunately, she "had a hard time in school." As she explained, "I would really struggle trying to get my grades up and yet I always got a lot of D's, my highest would be a C in school no matter how much I tried, no matter how much I studied. I've always had a hard time with it. It didn't come to me like it comes to a lot of kids." By the time she was in 8th grade, teachers and other students told her that she was "slow." Conveying the pain of this experience, Ayesha echoes Carol, who was also told that she was slow. With more support, Carol, whose comments about her son's struggles in school frame this chapter, was able to complete both high school and college. For Ayesha, the context of school stood in stark contrast to the caring environment her mother provided. Ayesha spent time with a number of friends who gave up on school and, influenced by them, she ultimately stopped trying. Eventually, she left school, had a child, and moved in with her grandmother, who was her only source of support.

Maya didn't reach high school because, as she put it, she "lost interest." As she reflected on her education, she considered elementary school to be the best years, recalling fondly a teacher who was "pretty stern" and her brother, who often helped her with homework. This teacher, she observed, was really the only adult in her life. She also recalls vividly a time when a teacher "paddled" her, an experience that was quite traumatic, especially because her aunt gave the teacher permission to do so. Ultimately, she explained that there was not enough work to keep her busy. "And that's what it was, it's like they didn't have enough, you know, enough work for me to keep me busy, so I just lost interest."

A common theme for many of the parents was the lack of support or care they received at school. Many of their parents struggled to make a living at a time when the economy was changing dramatically, and could not be a presence for their children. Moreover, for those women such as Amy, there were overwhelming responsibilities at home that precluded getting an education. After they became pregnant, there were few opportunities to get an education because schools were unprepared to meet their needs, particularly the flexibility that was required or the intellectual challenge that might have kept them in school. For that matter, school offered little support for Carol or Ayesha, who struggled and could not always keep up because they learned differently than the way their teachers expected them to learn. Teachers labeled them as "slow" in classes that treated difference as a deficit and where they felt vulnerable to personal criticism.

Few parents mentioned race explicitly in their accounts of school. Carol playfully recounted living and going to school in a White neighborhood where she was "pretty much the Black girl in a White neighborhood." Others took for granted that they grew up in segregated and deteriorating neighborhoods and attended majority-minority schools where they and their friends fell farther behind once they reached middle school. For Damian, who grew up in extreme poverty in the Robert Taylor Homes in Chicago, his identity as a young African American man was a source of both struggle and strength. His story is different than others', and illuminates some of the issues of race that are not highlighted in other parents' stories. Damian grew up with a single mother and nine siblings and once aspired to be a lawyer. He enjoyed school, he explained, because some of his teachers made learning fun, but he did not do as well as he would have liked: "Once I caught on and grasped what they were putting out, I enjoyed it." Damian recalled one teacher in particular who

> threw a dictionary in front of me and told me, "Okay, if you can't spell it, look it up in a dictionary." And I was thinking, "No one has ever taken the time to show me how to use a dictionary, so how am I going to find it in a dictionary?" And I'm gonna say right along 8th grade and 7th grade, all that started to turn around where the teachers were actually trying to find out what it is you know and what you don't know and then work with you.

Another teacher stood out for him, a teacher he had in summer school, who told Damian and his friends that, as African American males, they needed to work harder. His words resonated for Damian at the time, and do so even more now that he is a father.

> The way he put it out, it was in other words, even if you are doing B and A work, because you're an African American, you've still gotta do better. I was taught that because you're African American, or a Black male, that you gotta do better than your counterpart, which is a White guy beside you. And I can remember that just being instilled to me, even from my uncles and my older brothers, which has got ten years on me, telling you that yeah, this is what you have to do, otherwise you're not gonna make it.

Damian's recollections echo scholarship, which points out that Whiteness is a signifier for enfranchised, middle-class, influential families and children. For a father in Lewis's (2003) study, race is a significant factor. Facing racism will be one of his son's "greatest challenges . . . because this country is not set up for [African American] men to succeed" (p. 141). Lewis's research on race and schools may also shed some light on Damian's sense of regret when he thinks about his education. In the end, despite some positive experiences with teachers who reached out to him, "I just didn't do as well as I would liked to have done." In fact, he pointed out that he always felt he put in an "A" effort, but always ended up with "C's." Lewis (2003) offers one possible way to explain the disconnect that Damian identifies between his "effort" and the assessment of his work when she points out the extent to which schools place students of color at a disadvantage: "Language patterns and assessments of communicative competence affect whether children are heard and understood, whether they are read as cooperative and articulate, and also (because of the way it is delivered) what counts as knowledge in the classroom" (p. 69).

CREATING A CULTURE OF PARENT INVOLVEMENT AT IDA B. WELLS

As we have seen in Chapter 2, the principal at Ida B. Wells believed that parent involvement could help improve students' academic performance. Underlying such an effort was a set of widely held assumptions based on extensive research (e.g., Lee & Bowen, 2006):

- Active involvement of parents in schools is crucial to children's academic success

- Parent involvement is positively related to children's educational performance and may mediate the effects of poverty, parents' educational achievement, and race/ethnicity on achievement
- Increasing parent involvement may be a possible strategy for reducing the achievement gap
- Parents' presence at school conveys to children that they are expected to do well.

The principal's response to students' low test scores was to implement a series of parent meetings and to help parents see the value of education. What she learned from parents' stories, such as those we hear in Chapter 2, was that parents did value education and were more involved than she could have imagined. These are the lessons she tried to impart to teachers at Ida B. Wells:

Teachers need to understand that what the parents are giving and what the teachers need are not the same. Too often, we think they're doing nothing and we have to really embrace what they are doing and then say here are some things I need for the school, you're gonna get them. Instead of saying you're doing nothing, recognize that they are involved, you know, that type of thing because [if teachers] don't see it doesn't mean it's not being done.

Based on what she learned, the principal tried to shift away from a paradigm of thinking at Ida B. Wells that equates difference with deficit. She also recognized that parents were involved, even when parents' strategies for supporting their children were not visible to teachers. Equally important, another administrator at Ida B. Wells underscored parents' history of schooling as a frame through which to understand who parents are and ways to reach out to them:

Many parents don't come to school because their own experience was not positive. So we have to, first of all, know that and then do what we can to make sure that we reverse that. We can't change it, but you can make sure that their teaching experiences are positive and maybe that becomes their main paradigm. What they think of as part of their school relationship.

To understand parents' experiences, for this administrator, means listening to parents' stories, appreciating differences in perspective, and developing a deep sense of empathy and trust. Parents' backgrounds are varied and demonstrate why it is important to listen to parents' stories, to understand the different ways they are involved, and to resist overgeneralizing about parents' educational and socioeconomic backgrounds.

CONVERSATION AND COMMUNICATION
IN THE PARENT-TEACHER CONFERENCE

Teachers at Ida B. Wells were expected to and did meet with parents in parent-teacher conferences at least twice during the academic year, although teachers also kept in touch with parents throughout the year by phone, with notes they sent home with their students, with newsletters, and with suggestions for how to help children develop skills in reading and math. The primary intent of each mode of communication was to keep parents informed. As one teacher explained, she contacts parents to share a problem, have a "conversation," or get a parent's signature. She also seems well aware of the value of balancing negative and positive messages.

> I do contact parents if I have a problem or if it's just for a good,
> you know, conversation or just something that's not a negative
> behavior so they do get notes from me and usually they're pretty
> good about responding back or if I have something I need them to
> sign, they usually are pretty good about signing things, returning it,
> conferences.

Describing the ways in which this teacher stays in touch with parents brings to mind an important distinction between conversation and communication. Earlier, I used the notion of conversation to convey a sense of reciprocity, dialogue, empathy, and mutuality. Some teachers might attach a similar meaning to communication, but, for the most part, teachers' efforts to communicate entailed informing parents about events, field trips, weekly curriculum issues, ways to help with homework, and the like. Seen in this way, communication typically occurred in one direction. Communication is an iterative process, and it was difficult for teachers to know whether parents received the information at all or what parents paid attention to. After all, reading is a complex, interpretive act that includes applying prior knowledge to what may or may not be new information, organizing this information, and drawing inferences.

I make this distinction between conversation and communication to set the context for describing a parent-teacher meeting that was the source of some frustration for the teacher quoted above. The parent brought up a subject that this teacher had explained in the newsletter that she sent home, and the teacher wondered why this was a point of conversation now:

> I informed them of that, and I told her every week. Every single week . . . for the past nine weeks. So it's a little frustrating. You know, here I am, I'm trying to let them know, here, this is what your child's going to be working on this week. Help them at home. Telling time. We're working on contractions this week. So that in their newsletter says it all and so that was really disappointing and discouraging to me last week because she had no idea.

The teacher focuses on the information she provided in the newsletter and her sense of disappointment that this parent apparently "had no idea" of what the teacher had written. This was exemplified by the teacher's sustained focus on "I" and a set of assertions of what she did: "I informed," "I send a newsletter," "I state," and "I am trying to let them know." However, it's altogether possible that parents pay little attention to notifications that are one-directional because they offer no space for conversation.

Face-to-face meetings like this one offer the potential for dialogue, for sharing concerns, and for learning. However, the parent did not respond to the teacher's queries about why she was not aware of what, for the teacher, was clearly stated in the newsletter. The parent's silence fueled the teacher's puzzlement. She was clearly uncertain about how to interpret this silence.

> I did explain to her that I've been sending home newsletters and she avoided the questions, so I don't know if she was upset that her son maybe didn't give it to her or she'd seen it and just not read it, so one of two things could have easily happened.

Unfortunately, the teacher did not pursue the conversation, making this meeting a missed opportunity.

Another teacher explained that she "realizes that some parents are reluctant to talk with [her] because they might be self-conscious about their language abilities or they might just be nervous." And still another teacher suggested that parents' silence in parent-teacher meetings reflects parents' lack of "comfort." This same teacher observed, "I think the more comfortable a parent feels, I think the more interaction you're going to have with them. And the more interaction you have with a parent I think the more successful your children are gonna be in your class." In making this observation, this latter teacher not only affirmed the potential benefits of parent involvement on children's learning, but she also pointed to the value of consistency in parent-teacher interactions. Comfort derives from having a series of "interactions" that are meaningful to parents.

Parents may feel vulnerable, uncertain, and anxious at parent-teacher meetings because they are not familiar with what is expected of them. For parents, silence can represent respect and it is not their place to challenge teachers. Silence can also be a protective strategy against uncertainty about the role parents can and should play. These roles are not always spelled out in school. Without prior experiences, it is not clear if parents are to listen, observe, or participate. Dialogue, or the kind of "interaction" the teacher above describes, exists in response to things that have been said before and in anticipation of future interactions. As a result, all language is dynamic, relational, and engaged in a mutually reciprocal way. However, many parents are not accustomed to the give-and-take of ideas with teachers—with any educators—and there is often not a history that has conditioned them to believe that their ideas matter. Rarely are parents asked what they think. Moreover, the iterative nature of communication through notes, newsletters, and the like reinforces parents' role as receivers of information. They are neither collaborators, partners, nor decision-makers. In some cases, teachers may prefer it this way, and one teacher in Graue and Hawkins's (2010) study explained that communication is "best limited to one-way flows of information with parents needing to understand the practices of the school and teachers' assessments of their children, so that they can provide homework (and maybe disciplinary) support at home" (pp. 109–110; see also Dudley-Marling, 2009).

Despite the seeming neutrality of schools, there are ideological assumptions built into their very architecture that symbolize who speaks and who is the source of knowledge, expertise, and authority. The hierarchical relationship between students and teachers is inscribed in the traditional layout of classrooms, where students face the teacher in seating arrangements that dictate the flow of information and establish the teacher's authority and expertise. Moreover, the right-to-voice assumed by teachers and the absence of voice given to parents and families underscore the unequal relations of power that position parents and families as outsiders. Parents often come into school for parent-teacher conferences with a harried look, some coming from work, others from another school, and still others worry that they are already running late for their meeting with an older child's teacher a half-hour away. They are unsure where their child's teacher's room is. Some have not been in the school before and there are no signs that tell parents where the classrooms are. They ask for help or they wander the halls until they find the right classroom. Parents enter this setting without a map or guidebook, and much seems foreign to them. As Pushor (2010) points out, "Educators are positioned as holders of knowledge: of curriculum programming; of school policies, procedures, and practices; of children, teaching, and learning; and of appropriate expectations . . ." (p. 6). The implied role of parents is to support teachers' agenda.

Parents often do not feel comfortable in school for any number of reasons, not the least of which is that they can often feel like outsiders, and the anxiety of their past experiences often wells up as they face a teacher for the first time. Meeting with teachers is part of a ritual that begins with a welcoming gesture or smile followed by the teacher's assessment of a child's performance and often ends quickly with a list of skills that the parent can help the child work on. And then the teacher asks, "Do you have any questions for me?" A quiet uneasiness fills the room because no one has ever really asked parents what they think or to ask a question of a teacher. More often than not, parents have told me that they hear a teacher's evaluation of their child as a criticism of their parenting skills, and their silence can be interpreted as uneasiness and anxiety in an institutional space where parents themselves did not flourish. And yet, as we see in the exchange between parent and teacher above, it's possible to misread silence.

To address what silence means is to shift the focus away from the individual parent to the broader context of schooling, parents' histories, power, and the unequal playing field of parent-teacher relationships. I am reminded by Schultz's (2009) thoughtful research about silence and how easily teachers draw inferences about silence in classrooms. Schultz explains the logic of silence as a productive strategy that students use to protect themselves in sensitive conversations that may make them vulnerable to criticism or that might compromise the sense of identity they want to project. Schultz's point, one that is relevant to parent involvement, is that it would be a mistake to construe silence as a lack of attention, interest, knowledge, or disengagement. As she indicates, these are familiar social categories that offer explanations of why parents may be unresponsive, but they obscure how silence operates within a broader sociopolitical context that has excluded parents of color.

At times, silence reflects an individual's choice, but it is also reasonable to attribute silence to the normative and highly ritualized practice (Lawrence-Lightfoot, 2003) of parent-teacher conferences in which parents and teachers are not on equal footing. Language itself can be a limiting factor. Silence can mean that someone needs more time to reflect and put thoughts into words. Ultimately, it is important to consider who is silent and why and to understand different cultural practices that might influence parents' sense of deference to authority through silence. At the same time, resisting the inclination to overgeneralize about low-income parents of color, educators can begin to understand different cultural practices without overgeneralizing about low-income parents' beliefs, values, styles of communicating, language use, and behaviors (Gutiérrez & Rogoff, 2003). As I have suggested earlier in this book, cultural practices are rooted in shared social and historical experiences.

One teacher sought to create a level of "comfort" so that parents might feel more at home in the school—she clearly understood that parents often feel like unwelcome guests in a setting where there are very few educators who are people of color:

> I guess it's probably the parents' comfort level at school and if they're comfortable coming into the environment, and I know that's been an issue here. Parents haven't said that to me but we've heard in general they're just not comfortable. They don't feel welcome when they come in the school.

This teacher's focus on comfort reflects teachers' efforts to create a hospitable environment without necessarily recognizing the extent to which teachers' social status and position of authority reaffirm the power differential between themselves and parents. This power differential is intrinsic not only to the type of interpersonal interactions that occur during a parent-teacher conference, as just one example, but in the very structure of the school itself. Still, there is a more nuanced way to conceive of hospitality as a basis for developing the tools for interrogating the boundaries that separate teachers and parents. *Hospitality* is a word that is used to describe human behavior that has the potential to bring about understanding among strangers who do not share a common culture (Greene & Lidinsky, 2011), even if it is not altogether possible to eliminate the power differential that is inherent in the relationships between parents and teachers. To bring about this kind of understanding entails sharing stories that make explicit the values and beliefs that parents and educators embrace and that create intimacy among strangers. Such intimacy creates spaces of possibility and the grounds for conversation, understanding, and reciprocity based on trust, particularly when educators and parents acknowledge and respect differences.

To bridge the chasm (as teachers in Chapter 1 might describe it) between parents and educators requires empathy. This ability to "think what it would be like to be in the shoes of a person different from oneself" (Nussbaum, 1997, p. 269) is especially important given one teacher's sense that parents and teachers "really want the same thing." However, parents and teachers at Ida B. Wells did not share the same understanding of how increased testing and a developing magnet school program affected children and families, nor did they experience the effects of economic development in the same way given their differences in social status. Indeed, parents were adversely affected by policies that fragmented their neighborhood and community ties to Ida B. Wells. These are the differences that contribute to the gap between parents and educators. The alternative is to more fully understand the context of parents' lives as a significant part of the learning dynamic in schools—not as something that needs to be overcome. Moreover, rather than see information flowing from schools to parents, knowledge about one's family and community can be part of a reciprocal process of information flowing across multiple pathways that connect home, school, and community (Weiss et al., 2009).The challenges that White teachers face in the racially coded spaces of school are seemingly intractable. As Lawrence-Lightfoot puts it, "When parents whose values, histories, and life circumstances are more similar to the teacher's, this trading of places is easier, more familiar, and natural. For others, the teacher needs to listen harder—to the text and subtext—of what is being said and stretch to make an empathic connection" (p. 103). In the end, we might consider Anzaldua's (2007) metaphor of a "borderland" to describe this mutual respect for differences and reciprocity and where she says "the space between individuals shrinks with intimacy" (p. 19). We begin to witness spaces of possibility in the parent meetings that the principal at Ida B. Wells instituted, in which parents and educators were learning about the assumptions they each had about one another and developing mutually respectful ways to work with one another to help children learn. That parents and educators began to work with one another as partners in a collaborative relationship stemmed from ongoing, consistent leadership from the principal who made relationships between parents and teachers a priority. In turn, parents began to re-examine their roles as supporters and advocates, even while recognizing the uneven playing field between themselves and their children's teachers.

RE-IMAGINING SCHOOLS AS INCLUSIVE AND DEMOCRATIC SPACES

We all have a tendency to designate spaces, neighborhoods, and communities that mark the people who occupy them as different. As I have suggested earlier in this chapter, differences in learning or approaches to parent involvement can easily be cast as deficits. Although the social categories we use are rhetorical constructions, they shape, even limit, the ways many of us think about the families who inhabit these spaces and attend schools. The opinions that teachers form have significant implications for their expectations of the students who live in particular neighborhoods, the construction of curriculum, the distribution of funding, and reform efforts (Buendia, Ares, Juarez, & Peercy, 2004) often aimed at mitigating the effects of poverty. Thus, low-income students find themselves in special tutorials and remedial programs that are isolated spatially from other classrooms, that influence the ways children see themselves, and that contribute to the reproduction of inequality. Teaching low-status knowledge in low-track classrooms reproduces inequality by limiting children's access to the kind of knowledge they will need to excel in school. Unfortunately, these rhetorical designations (i.e., urban, low-income) allow teachers and administrators to name the experiences of children and families without having to invoke the politically charged language of race and class. Thus educators place low-income children of color in low-track classrooms in disproportionate numbers, where they can easily languish.

The parents whose voices fill the pages of *Race, Community, and Urban Schools* remind us that their own experiences were no different, and that their own teachers often gave up on them. Meanwhile, middle-class White students often have access to rich, complex curricula that will prepare them to enter magnet programs. The result is a further instance of the kind of spatial inequality to which I have called attention throughout this volume—which exacerbates the Black-White achievement gap or the education debt that finds its source in the unequal distribution of resources in schools and the neighborhood spaces that children occupy with their families.

Race is indeed part of the everyday life of a school and parents' efforts to navigate their roles in helping their children gain access to opportunity. Institutions such as schools are embedded with cultural values and power and, as I indicate in Chapter 1, Critical Race Theory foregrounds the conflicts that people of color face in school, where they are often marginalized in discussions of mandated testing, curriculum, classroom instruction, and policy (Barton et al., 2004). Thus Tillman (2004) not only attributes African American families' lack of engagement in school to differences in race and class, but to adversarial relationships between home and school that find their source in the unequal power relationships between parents and teachers. Moreover, she points to work schedules that conflict with meetings at school, lack of transportation, miscommunication between school and home, and the ways in which schools solicit their involvement. Unfortunately, social, contextual, and cultural factors are treated as external factors that need to be dealt with outside of the classroom. Indirectly, students who come from families with fewer complicating factors are given unfair advantage.

For Tillman and others (Lareau, 2003; Lareau & Horvat, 1999; Lewis, 2003), race and class reproduce inequality, particularly through the ways in which educators marginalize and potentially silence low-income minority parents. As a consequence, families whose children most need support in school are the very families who are least likely to have opportunities to partner with teachers, serve as decision-makers, or collaborate (Noguera, 2001). This lack of decision-making power contributes to the sociopolitical debt that Ladson-Billings (2006) describes to explain the extent to which Black, Latina/o, and other families of color have had little "franchise" on school policy. The effect is to exclude families of color from a democratic decision-making process that affects their children's ability to attend quality schools.

The parents whose stories I tell confront inequalities and colliding expectations when they come to school. They have long held the view that public education can level the playing field with its promise of equal access and opportunity. Indeed, Dewey had expressed his optimism that education could serve as a "fundamental method of social progress and reform" (cited in Lawrence-Lightfoot, 2003). However, his optimism has not been realized in schools that reproduce inequality instead of giving students access to the knowledge and skills that are needed to function effectively within a democratic society (Kinloch, 2012). Similarly, Marian Wright Edelman (2012) cites a recent Civil Rights Data Collection survey to explain persistent "[i]nequities in school funding and educational resources [that] place students of color in low-performing schools with inadequate resources and often ineffective teachers." Unfortunately, parents' expectations for equality and opportunity and disappointments "shape parental expectations and influence the ways relationships are negotiated between families and schools" (Lawrence-Lightfoot, 2003, p. 113). As long as policy-makers limit reform to curriculum and teaching and resist developing economic and social programs, there is little hope for equity (Berliner, 2014; Rothstein, 2004).

CONCLUSION

Parent involvement alone will not address the problems that maintain inequality. However, changing the nature of social interaction in schools can help us reimagine schools as both inclusive and democratic spaces. Indeed, a dialogic conception of parent involvement that is relational provides the conditions of possibility for creative practice—practice that challenges normative conceptions of institutional spaces that reproduce inequality and the constructions of "us" and "them." Place does not need to be exclusionary, marked by permanence and boundedness, but can encompass openness and change, constructed by people in social interaction with one another, marked by reciprocity and a more equitable distribution of power. Thus re-imagining the institution of school in this way allows us to see place as a dynamic, constantly evolving network of new possibilities. As Cresswell (2004) has observed, "Places are never finished but [are] always the result of processes and practices. As such, places need to be studied in terms of the 'dominant institutional projects,' the individual biographies of people negotiating a place, and the way in which a sense of place is developed through the interaction of structure and agency" (p. 37). In the end, policies are made and, as such, they can change to give advantage to all children and families.

CHAPTER 5

Families as Advocates in Creating Spaces of Hope at Home, in Schools, and in the Community

> We would like to see school-sponsored programs where parents and teachers can meet together to talk genuinely about how parents can help with home literacy and school events. Not all parents can be involved at school, but we need to know specific ways we can help as partners in our children's education.
>
> —Excerpt from Parents' Letter to the Editor, local newspaper

> I can't accept that kids are troubled. I know a lot of these kids and their families. I grew up here.
>
> —Richard, parent at Ida B. Wells

Throughout this book, I have challenged a dominant narrative that portrays low-income African American families as detached and uninvested in their children's education. Such a narrative is fueled by traditional conceptions of parent involvement that limit parents' roles to very specific types of support, including helping in classrooms, accompanying children on field trips, or participating in school events and PTAs. Large-scale research conducted soon after the Coleman Report (1966) appeared has also tended to overgeneralize the characteristics of low-income families by ignoring the complexities of families' lives, how race is lived in schools, and the roles that parents play in supporting their children at home. A Critical Race Theory perspective throws into relief the extent to which state-sponsored discrimination in housing, employment, and education has disenfranchised people of color and limited families' access to opportunities that enable children to flourish. Thus, Ladson-Billings (2006) has re-cast policy-makers' descriptions of the Black-White achievement gap as an "education debt" and a "sociopolitical debt" to call attention to the historical inequities that have muted the voices of African American, Latina/o, and other minority families in decisions that affect their children.

Re-casting the problem as an education debt shifts the focus of blame for underachievement from individual responsibility, especially families, to broader structural explanations to understand the persistence of low-income minority students' underachievement in school. For example, why is it that schools aren't meeting kids' needs? A CRT perspective prompts us to look for answers in the history of race in our country and the way in which racial inequality reproduces itself. The implications of this racial history are clear. A failure to provide African American children with access to quality education and resources has prevented youth from gaining access to an education that equips them with the skills they need for "political and civil involvement" in the 21st century (Winn & Behizadeh, 2011, p. 149). Unless educators and policy-makers deal openly and honestly with race, we may very well keep repeating the cycles of exclusion evident in the stories parents tell in this book.

AFRICAN AMERICAN FAMILIES AND EDUCATION

The history of African Americans' struggle to gain access to quality education has much to teach us about the significant role that parents and teachers played in making decisions that affect children's lives. In fact, initiatives to involve African American families in school now represent efforts that were very much in place for generations. Specifically, the history of African American parent involvement before desegregation provides a counternarrative rooted in an ethic of care and dignity that served to lift up the community, not just individual students (Delpit, 2012; Perry, Steele, & Hilliard III, 2003). Tillman (2004) explains that

> African American parent involvement in the pre-*Brown* era of education represented, to a great extent, a framework for parental involvement that was largely based on cultural and community values, a shared sense of responsibility, and a strong desire for social and academic excellence for African American children. The activism of parents also represented a political aspect of parent involvement. (p. 166)

With desegregation and school districts' strong resistance to *Brown*, in both North and South, "children were placed in a racist context" (Edwards, 1993, p. 142) and, as Tillman points out, African American parents were the "uninvited guests in their children's schooling." Unfortunately, many African American families' proactive involvement was transformed and replaced by "cynicism, withdrawal, and pessimism" (p. 167). Edwards and her colleagues (2010) contend that reform movements in education continue to ignore the sociocultural factors that have had detrimental effects on families of color. These factors and a changing political economy are as important, if not more so, to understanding persistent inequality as the unintended consequences of the *Brown* decision.

This kind of cynicism, withdrawal, and pessimism plays out in Jonathon Kozol's (1967) story in *Death at an Early Age*, published just a year before the Coleman report. *Death at An Early Age* is a story of African American families who cared deeply about the effects of segregation on their children's ability to learn, the inequitable distribution of resources, and a deficit-driven curriculum that perpetuated the myth of African American inferiority. Kozol also tells the story of African American parents' efforts to gain community control of education. They protested at the school through sit-ins and at times even disrupted classes. Parents marched in an effort to change the egregious conditions at the school where Kozol taught, but the superintendent rebuffed their efforts and dismissed them summarily as a "stain" on the streets in the neighborhood.

It is a story that repeated itself in the case of Ocean Hill-Brownsville in Brooklyn, New York, in 1968. Fisher (2009) points out that "With a mostly Black student body and largely White teaching staff and administration, Black youth and their parents were becoming increasingly wary of the curriculum and pedagogical practices employed by public schools" (p. 56). Students wanted to see images of themselves in the curriculum and parents felt that teachers did not believe in their children's ability to learn. With increasing pressure from African American and Latina/o families, Ocean Hill-Brownsville was an experiment to decentralize three elementary, one intermediate, and one middle school and give over economic and staff decisions to a locally controlled board made up of African American and Latina/o parents, church leaders, and community residents who believed that educators were not responsive to their needs. The assumption was that local control of key decisions would improve the quality of education in this low-income neighborhood, but controversy emerged with the transfer of 18 teachers and a strike precipitated by the United Federation of Teachers (Noguera, 2001). In the end, what started as a movement to meet the needs of underserved students resulted in anger, frustration, and parents' distrust of public schools.

Fisher (2009) chronicles the emotional and political upheaval surrounding these events in Ocean Hill-Brownsville, as well as the consequences. In documenting this period in the 1960s and 1970s, she argues that parents' actions reflected African Americans' profound historical commitment to education and literacy as the foundation for collective action, self-reliance, and dignity. Since the time of slavery, African American families have used literacy as a political form of voice and a means for freedom, yet Fisher points out that efforts to educate African American children in the mechanics of reading and writing, to "leave no child behind" in this current era of standards and accountability, are divorced from this legacy of using literacy as a way to "write their way to freedom" (Fisher, 2009, p. 114).

The Black News, a community newspaper in Ocean Hill-Brownsville, helped parents become aware of additional opportunities that helped open doors for themselves and their children, "to propel Black youth, parents, and educators" to address "issues of mis-education" in public schools and meet the needs of Black and Puerto Rican students in "Independent Black Institutions" and schools in particular (Fisher, 2009, p. 57). Parent involvement was a primary focus of *The Black News,* not simply in the ways that parents supported their children's education, but in the formation of adult programs designed to help parents transform the inequitable conditions in the segregated schools of New York. One such example was the Black Study Circle, a group that provided opportunities for adults to discuss Black history and literature and other related topics in "small learning communities" and emphasized mutual learning, support, and collaboration in advancing the common good of the community (pp. 71–72). In relevant instances, adults took on the responsibility of helping one another with reading and writing. In turn, adults were in a position to instill pride in their children with knowledge about African American history, literature, and the arts and debunk a persistent myth of inferiority promulgated in public schools. Parent organizations such as the Parent Association of P.S. 305 were determined to make sure that parents knew their rights and felt empowered to adopt an aggressive, activist stance toward the education of their children, as well as foster dignity, self-reliance, and independence.

The act of recovery in rewriting historical narratives about African American literacy practices such as Fisher's, among others (e.g., McHenry, 2002; Richardson, 2003), reminds us that the stories we tell are part of an ongoing struggle that involves "power and positionings" (Compton-Lilly, 2007): whose story gets told, who gets to tell that story, and what is left out. Unfortunately, the "quest for access to literacy is a story that is not necessarily found in history books, and the story changes depending on the storyteller's experiences" (Edwards, McMillon, & Turner, 2010, p. 17). Counternarratives of parents' and other family members' commitment to education challenge a dominant narrative that silences their voices in maintaining the *status quo* and privilege in schools. Parents' responses give voice to the African American experience and reflect resiliency, self-reliance, and resistance to unjust practices. If African American parents lack the sense of connectedness they once had to schools, it is not from a lack of resolve to help their children succeed amidst poverty and a political economy that has exacerbated inequality in African American neighborhoods.

Separate has never meant equal. Inequities in education laid the foundation for economic inequality (Theoharis, 2013). Still, historians (Anderson, 1988; Cecelski, 1994) and educators (Walker, 1996) alike have demonstrated that many Black schools flourished, despite the lack of resources, materials, and facilities. Poor conditions alone could not limit many African American teachers' and parents' efforts to educate children by holding them to rigid standards and enhancing their self-worth within a supportive community. Black schools nourished children's minds and souls with an ethic of care borne out of a collective struggle to improve the condition of their lives. "During segregation," Wright (2004) observed, "the black community, left to its own resources, was able to create and sustain a culture of learning . . . where the focus was on learning and the associated responsibility for one's own effort in the learning process" (pp. 100–101). Edwards's (1993) view is that integration "eroded much cultural strength among African American communities at the cost of the goal of equity in education" (p. 347). Walker (1996), too, has observed that children in many of these schools simply did not have the option of failing. Ministers, parents, and teachers expected children to succeed. The network of excellent schools that developed after 1925 throughout the South may have been one of the unintended consequences of Jim Crow.

Historians have not only chronicled the extent to which African American parents have been at the center of initiatives to build excellent schools, but demonstrated the extent to which they were also at the center of resistance to desegregation (Cecelski, 1994). It was clear that if integration were to occur at all after 1954, African American students would have to attend White schools. This meant that Black schools would close and African American teachers would lose their jobs. Efforts to desegregate resulted in the loss of the strong sense of community that peers, teachers, and parents worked so hard to create, the collective memory that instilled pride and character, and the sense that one's future was inextricably tied to others (Delpit, 2012; see also Perry, Steele, & Hilliard, 2003). Still, it would be a mistake to misinterpret the value historians have placed on all-Black schools. No one would argue that this was a golden age of education or that this is something to which we should return (Payne, 2008).

Unfortunately, efforts to integrate schools ignored the broader sociocultural facets of desegregation that exacerbated inequality (Irvine

& Irvine, 1983), and these efforts to create change have been stymied in a persistently racist society evident in the resegregation of schools (Kozol, 2005; Orfield, 1997), the achievement gap, the dropout rate, and the education-to-prison pipeline (Winn & Behizadeh, 2011). Teachers assume that African American parents are uninterested in their children's literacy achievement when they do not participate in events at school, that they lack the capacity to help their children with reading, and that they lack the appropriate parenting skills. One teacher I spoke with explained that "The parents, if the grandparents don't think that education is important, and then the parents don't see it, as an important element, then, you know, that goes down to the kids and maybe that's why. Seems like it must be some kind of a cycle, I'm guessing." However, the view that many parents or grandparents do not think education is important or do not care runs counter to what is known about African American family life and the values placed on education (Edwards et al., 2010). Without such a perspective, teachers translate differences in parent involvement as deficits, not recognizing that "parents are unable to successfully participate in literacy interactions valued in schools" (p. 103) or that low-income African American families support their children in alternative ways.

PARENT INVOLVEMENT IN A CHANGING POLITICAL ECONOMY

A changing political economy has exacerbated inequality by draining urban neighborhoods of necessary resources and eliminating vital public services that low-income families have relied on as a firewall against the effects of poverty. This redistribution of resources has placed an enormous burden on low-income households. Ironically, the rhetoric surrounding "parental choice" in education simply ignores the ways that the application of market economic principles to education has marginalized the families that policy-makers seek to empower with choice programs and vouchers. Moreover, neoliberal policies that enforce increased standards and accountability have placed low-income students of color at a distinct disadvantage by limiting instruction to remediation and the acquisition of basic skills based on autonomous models of literacy. Schools rely on such a model in the widespread use of programmed instruction and worksheets aimed at fostering comprehension and achievement on standardized tests. This was particularly evident for students such as Minelik, whose struggles in school I documented in Chapter 3. However, autonomous models of literacy ignore the deeply contextualized and ideological nature of literacy and the range of literacies that youth enact in their day-to-day experiences (e.g., Kinloch, 2010). Indeed, students placed in low-track classes are more often than not ill-prepared to become part of an information economy based on technology and critical literacy. In this way, schools reproduce inequality and students enter a workforce that is already stratified by race and class.

In Chapters 2 and 3, I presented specific examples and evidence of the varied roles that parents have played in their children's education within the context of spatial inequality. We learn about the spaces that parents create at home to nurture their children's education, the value parents place on community and family, and the extent to which parents support their children's learning by fostering their children's sense of belonging, independence, and resilience. In Chapters 2 and 3 I highlighted the ways in which parents and children co-construct the roles that parents play to support their children's education. Their relationship is reciprocal in the sense that parents adopt roles that they believe they can and should play; at the same time, children express needs that inform the ways their parents respond as both supporters and advocates. Thus, parents supported their children when they believed the pace of instruction ignored their children's rhythm of development and learning or when they believed they needed to bolster their children's sense of self-worth.

Moreover, we learn in Chapter 4 that parents approached their children's education with a sense of urgency. Parents were committed to supporting their children's education as a way to ensure their children's economic well-being. These parents had faith in schools despite their own life histories, which underscores the extent to which teachers failed them when they were in school. Because these parents' teachers often treated difference as a deficit and lacked an ethic of care that might have kept them in school longer, parents such as Richard and Damian were particularly vigilant about holding teachers accountable to make sure that teachers attended to their children's needs. This was even more the case when parents learned in parent meetings (Chapter 2) the discrepancy between children's grades and children's performance on standardized tests. These meetings gave parents a space where they could exchange ideas with other parents, express their concerns to teachers, and develop a network of support to begin advocating for their children. Finally, parent meetings enabled the principle at Ida B. Wells to recognize parents' capacities for supporting their children's education (Long, 2011).

Parent meetings provided a curricular space that called attention to a disconnect between teachers' definitions of how parents should be involved in their children's education and the real-life skills and attributes that parents are trying to teach their children. There was also a different kind of disconnect that forced me to reflect on my own assumptions about school. That is, as educators, we may not fully realize the importance of parents' backgrounds and don't make an effort to discuss these histories with parents. Without these kinds of conversations, it is possible to assume some sort of deficit perspective that diminishes the ways that parents support and advocate for their children.

As I suggested in Chapter 1, language serves as an interpretive frame that influences the ways that teachers interact with parents and the expectations they hold for the students in their classrooms. The metaphors that teachers adopt also reaffirm the extent to which the relationships between parents and teachers are rife with power and privilege in educational spaces that treat parents as strangers (Chapter 4). Clearly, parent involvement does not exist on an even playing field. Rather, teachers' expertise is often given more legitimacy over parents' knowledge and experience. Therefore, I worry that it's possible to silence parents by adopting a one-way model of communication rather than engaging in a two-way conversation with parents. I have seen how easy it is to equate parents' silence as a lack of care, detachment, or lack of investment in children's education rather than a response to the power differential between parents and teachers as a source of parents' silence.

Absent in my conversations with teachers is a sense of how state-sponsored discrimination and a changing political economy have created a burden on families and limited families' access to resources. Still, parents' stories reveal the ways that agency, structure, and culture interact, allowing parents to create positive changes for themselves and their children despite the economic challenges they confront.

Change begins when, as White teachers, we interrogate our own sense of power and privilege and reach across difference toward racial and cultural understanding. Culture encompasses families' lived experiences and practices—their beliefs, values, worldview, communication style, expectations, social interaction, self-presentation, and cognitive processing—that give meaning to their lives (Howard, 2010). However, culture is dynamic and changes, bound by neither race nor ethnicity. People have "cultural repertoires" (Gutiérrez, 2011) that are shaped by the communities of practice they inhabit, including geography, families, immigrant status, neighborhoods, places of worship, and school. Culture is also a product of historical, social, and political contexts. Therefore, it is important to understand the histories and valued practices of cultural groups without also essentializing differences. Meeting the needs of children and families cannot be accomplished with a one-size-fits-all program. To ignore the contexts of families' day-to-day lives is to fall prey to traditional models of parent involvement (e.g., Epstein, 2010).

I realize that the story of parent involvement that I tell in this book emerged within a specific context. Making parents' engagement visible will require multiple stories. After all, not all parents are like those whom I portray here or have access to the resources I describe. Still, I suggest that the story I tell has implications for the ways that parent support specialists, teachers, and teacher educators think about parent involvement in other educational spaces. As Graue and Hawkins (2010) point out, it is important that educators understand more fully who parents are and what they are already doing to support their children in order to develop models of parent involvement that are reciprocal and collaborative. Reciprocity requires that educators balance their own goals and expectations with parents' beliefs, values, and priorities. I highlighted in Chapter 4 that such a view of reciprocity is dialogic and requires that parents and educators listen respectfully to one another in order to collaborate in the best interests of children. This conversation is one in which individuals from different cultures can begin to cross over into one another's worlds in order to develop a greater sense of empathy for the silences that might puzzle us. Unfortunately, the tendency is to locate meaning in individual responsibility. Doing so, however, can obscure the broader contextual and structural issues that explain silence. If we fail to listen to parents in these ways, including their silence, then it is unlikely that we will be able to create meaningful partnerships with parents.

As I reflect on the realities in schools and the challenges that families confront in a changing political economy, I envision a model of parent involvement that is more expansive in its understanding of who parents are, what they want for their children, and what they want for themselves. I'd like to suggest that such a model be driven by a social justice framework that embraces (a) parents' sense of agency to envision and enact change, (b) the dignity of all families and the assets that they bring to their children's education, (c) the value of culturally relevant pedagogy to build upon the rich linguistic and cultural backgrounds of families, (d) an equitable distribution of resources among all people, and (e) the democratic participation of families who are partners, collaborators, and decision-makers in a collective effort with educators to help children flourish as good people who have the capacity to be critical, creative, and engaged citizens.

The model of parent involvement I point to in *Race, Community, and Urban Schools* is one way to work within the confines of a world where power differentials are inevitable: where parents and educators can begin to share power in a more democratic space in which parents and teachers collaborate as partners in making decisions about how to help children flourish; where parents and educators can question and unsettle dominant narratives that embrace deficit perspectives of low-income families of color; and where parents and educators examine who is accountable to whom in this partnership. These are ethical questions that have broad implications for parents and teachers who, in crossing the very real and imagined boundaries between home and school, need to "confront fears, biases, presuppositions, and power structures" that stand in the way of meaningful change and equity (Kinloch, 2012, p. 114).

In the remainder of this chapter, I want to highlight parents' voices and the importance of creating spaces where parents have opportunities to write, interrogate unquestioned assumptions about youth, and redefine their roles as parents. To do so, I return to the quotations that opened this chapter.

LITERACY, VOICE, AND COMMUNITY

The first quote is taken from a letter to the editor of a local newspaper in which parents whom I mentored at a local primary school responded to a letter that appeared in that same newspaper. In the letter that I shared with the parents, the writer had called attention to the state Superintendent of Public Instruction's threat to take over high schools that consistently fell short of meeting Annual Yearly Progress. This letter-writer also attributed the underachievement of students at these schools to parents who simply didn't care about their children's future. I wanted to know what the parents I worked with thought of such an argument. At my prompting, the seven parents who participated in weekly meetings that I led for 10 weeks wrote a letter to the editor to air their own opinion about the role that parents play in their children's education. In their letter, they criticized the assumption that students' low achievement in schools could be attributed to low-income parents' lack of involvement in their children's education. Not surprisingly, they believed that parents could serve as an important source of support for teachers, but they also needed guidance, as they wrote in their letter, through "school-sponsored programs where parents and teachers can meet . . . and specific ways we can help as partners in our children's education."

In their open letter to the Superintendent of Public Instruction, parents also shared their concerns about the quality of their children's education. All of the parents had attended one of the two schools that the State Superintendent had threatened to take over. They criticized the letter-writer's argument that a takeover would have the effect of destroying a well-established community surrounding each school. In fact, they questioned whether there had ever been a supportive community even when they attended these schools as students. Finally, the parents also called on teachers to make a stronger commitment to students of color, "students who are not like them," based on their own interactions with teachers in the past and present.

We recently read an opinion essay in the [local newspaper] and learned that the State Department of Education is considering taking over [two local high schools]. We want to thank you for your willingness to come in and help out our schools, which we understand have not met Annual Yearly Progress for the past few years. We are just as concerned as you are in having the local school corporation provide a growth plan for teaching and learning.

We want to know, too, that our children's teachers are holding all children to a high standard and that they are always looking for ways to improve their effectiveness with an ever-changing group of students who have different needs. We want to know that teachers refuse to surrender to the combined menaces of poverty, bureaucracy, and budgetary shortfall.

It will be important to see our children's scores improve; more importantly, we think teachers need to connect more with students who may not be like them. Although the author of the opinion essay expressed her concern that taking over schools will diminish a sense of community, we cannot say that there was much of a sense of community to begin with. Creating and sustaining a sense of community is essential. If our children feel they belong, then they will be in a better position to learn.

This letter reflects the emergence of these parents' public voice and their ability to use writing to interrupt a conversation that tended to marginalize, or even dismiss, their role in supporting their children's education. Parents stressed the value of community and urged teachers to forge relationships with their children by "connect[ing] more with students who may not be like them." They also echoed the letter writer's concern that teachers hold students to high expectations and not "surrender to the combined menaces of poverty, bureaucracy, and budgetary shortfall."

Together, the parents and I discussed what parents wanted readers to understand amid different and conflicting points of view. We met in two small groups to draft their argument and refine the letter's language and tone, which initially reflected the parents' anger and impatience with what they had read. As a group, we shared our drafts, and came to some consensus about the stance parents wanted to take, the tone that would best get their point across, and the language we would use to ensure that readers heard them. Therefore, they agreed to begin their letter by thanking the letter-writer and conveying their openness to the argument the letter writer made.

Ultimately parents wanted to stress the extent to which they were committed to their children's education and that they wanted teachers to hold high expectations for their children. They also felt strongly that teachers should respect children's ethnic, racial, and cultural backgrounds. Their concerns were warranted because up to 25% of students in area high schools may be graduating without achieving state standards. Students who received the waivers that allowed them to do so have been disproportionately African American and Latina/o and exceed state averages. Unfortunately, the issue has not been on the local school district's radar (Kilbride, 2012).

The experiences parents shared in a space that the principal set aside in the school provided the context where they could share ideas and form relationships with one another, and connect their worldviews to others around them. In turn, the bonds they created served as a supportive network that fueled their collective efforts to act upon their shared concerns (Lawson & Alameda-Lawson, 2012). Indeed, they began to develop an important source of social capital within a supportive network of other parents. Thus they could imagine a role for themselves as advocates for children in general, not just their own. One challenge is to build on the social capital that parents develop and connect parents to institutions that can provide access to resources that can enable them to leverage change. Seeing opportunities is the first step toward effecting change.

Indeed, naming the reality of their experiences in writing their response helped parents to understand the possibility of asserting their voices. To use Freire's words (1970), the parents' letter illustrated the ways in which they were beginning to "assert the right and responsibility to read, write, and transform their experiences, but to use literacy as a way to reconstitute their relationship to society . . . to const[ruct their] voice as part of a wider project of possibility and empowerment" (Giroux, 1987, p. 7). Specifically, literacy served as the ground for analysis, critique, and agency that manifested itself in their ability to engage purposefully and strategically in critical dialogue and resistance. However, as I have suggested in Chapter 2 and elsewhere, parents' developing sense of agency can be fragile, a work in progress. Therefore, it's one thing to provide parents with resources, including a space for critical reflection. My role as a mentor has taught me that it is another thing to support parents with the tools they say they need to help their children flourish in consistent, supportive ways built on trusting relationships that develop over time.

In the context of reading and writing, parents were also learning to understand the kinds of language and literacy experiences to look for in their children's classrooms and take a proactive role in asking questions of teachers and administrators about whether their children were receiving the kind of instruction they needed. As we see in the letter they wrote, parents wanted their children to do well in school; sometimes they are simply not sure what they can do to help.

CREATING PUBLIC SPACES

In this section, I shift to a different kind of conversation with three parents who have consistently attended parent meetings for more than 2 years. Richard and Marc are both participating in a program at Ida B. Wells that employs parents as assistants in 11 different schools. After spending most of their time in classrooms helping teachers, Richard and Marc discuss their surprise that young children in a primary school challenged their authority. Damian, who has entered the conversation, observes that some kids are just inherently "troubled." All three parents know one another well and feel comfortable challenging one another based on a history of shared experiences and trust.

> RICHARD: I can't accept that kids are troubled. I know a lot of these
> kids and their families. I grew up here.
> DAMIAN: That's just the way some of them are. I lived in Robert
> Taylor. And I could remember seeing some things that I thought
> a kid my age should have never seen. There was just a bad
> environment, extremely bad. I don't remember a lot of it, but I
> remember some of the fires and there was just a lot of stuff that
> went on in the community so we couldn't always go outside. We
> would always have to stay in the house.
> RICHARD: You're saying that it's who they are.
> MARC: You see the way some of these kids act, the way they talk to us.
> I had a kid come up and say things. If that were my child . . .
> RICHARD: But I don't think they're troubled. Like it's who they are.
> No one is troubled. [He points to himself as if to say no one is
> troubled inside.]
> DAMIAN: I don't know how you can say that. I grew up in the streets
> and saw lots of stuff. It's their home life. Their parents aren't
> strict enough with them. They don't have anyone who cares.
> How you carry yourself.
> MARC: I've seen that too. I grew up in it. A lot of negativity. I think a
> lot of it has to do with the environment in the neighborhood that
> they're being brought up in, um, let alone at home. Some of the
> things that they're, you know, doing or acting out in school is
> just a mirror or reflection of what they're seeing at home in a lot
> of cases.
> RICHARD: I know. I just don't agree.
> DAMIAN: It's their upbringing. You know I am strict with my girls.
> RICHARD: I think it has a lot to do with not having a place to go. They
> just hang out. But look. The churches are always locked. That's

wrong. They should have a place where they can go and hang out, maybe get some help with school, and play even at night. Parents should have a place to go. We could be there and meet with parents and give them advice about how to help. We could start something.

Marc and Damian nod in agreement, but they are unsure about how Richard's idea of creating a parent center could become a reality. The building Richard referred to was an old church several miles from Ida B. Wells where the police chief had developed a boxing program for teens. The church sat across from Richard's home in a neighborhood where there were a number of abandoned houses. There was also a community garden, but the signs pointed to a city that had begun to ignore the part of the city where Richard lived with his wife and six school-aged children. The lack of development in Richard's neighborhood is symptomatic of how an inequitable distribution of resources contributes to spatial inequality related to race, place, and power.

Low-income neighborhoods that house families of color experience little or no growth, thus limiting access to what youth and their families need in order to flourish. In this specific context that Richard mentions, there are no bookstores, coffee shops, or grocery stores where people can gather, talk, and develop a sense of community. There are no parks that have lighting where children can play after school. In addition, without reliable means of transportation, it is difficult for children to attend after-school tutoring and enrichment programs. And as I mention in Chapter 2, parents called attention to the increased fragmentation of the community.

It is significant that the debate among three African American fathers, all struggling economically, focused on race, identity, power, and place. As an African American father, Marc has turned his own life around and put what he referred to as the "negativity" of drugs and violence of his youth behind him. He knows people change and his children served as an impetus for that change. In Chapter 2, he describes the child he tutors, and he explains that he takes his children to the homeless center to show his children the value of civic engagement and giving back to the community. He also instills in them a profound sense of faith. Richard, too, has grown up in similar circumstances and recognizes the ways that the environment exerts its influence by isolating youth who need to have a sense of belonging and identity in a place where they feel at home. For him, youth may be troubled, but he would never consider that what they experience is an indelible part of who they are. After all, Richard grew up in a neighborhood like the one where he lives now, dropped out of high school to start a family, and matured. He sees himself in the youth that Damian referred to as "troubled" and can't accept Damian's explanation. As I discuss in Chapter 1, the labels that teachers use, such as "urban" and "poor," have staying power and not only limit how they see youth but how youth begin to see themselves. If parents and teachers begin to see youth as troubled, then it is likely that we will look past the assets and talents that youth possess.

Not unlike the parents' letter, this conversation among three African American fathers helps to broaden the notion of parent involvement. Their exchange foregrounds the kind of advocacy with which parents can support children's growth and development not only in school, but also in the community. Evident in the conversation is the interplay of ideas, analysis, and critique of power that gives meaning to what I have referred to as spaces of hope. For Kinloch (2012), critique represents a form of "democratic engagement" and promotes a questioning frame of mind that can lead to a more just, humane, and equitable world. Such a view challenges traditional conceptions of parents' roles and affirms the importance of providing spaces for these kinds of "democratic engagements." Formal and informal opportunities like these open up a conversation about how to leverage power and resources to create substantive change and equity. As Freire (1974) points out, the more opportunities people have to "review critically their past and present experiences in and with the world, the more they realize that the world is not a cul-de-sac for men and women, an unalterable state which crushes them" (p. 137). As educators, we can ensure that parents have spaces where they can develop the tools, language, and capital to challenge the status quo in schools and in the community.

Unfortunately, privatization, a hallmark of neoliberal economic policy, has eroded the use of public spaces and works against a vision of community, solidarity, and egalitarianism. Parents in Chapter 2 made clear that gentrification has torn apart the fabric of their neighborhood where the boundary between relative wealth and poverty has become more apparent. And at the time I was finishing *Race, Community, and Urban Schools*, the city had begun to demolish some of the vacant, dilapidated rental properties surrounding Ida B. Wells, which were deemed unsafe for investment. What remains are the visible scars of change that have covered over the day-to-day lives of families who at one time contributed to the vitality of a neighborhood school. Developers have placed a chain-link fence around a concrete playground, children don't feel safe playing in what little green space exists, and speculators have begun to buy rental properties with the prospect of making a profit when the city's gentrification moves farther south past Ida B. Wells (see Figure 2.1). Unfortunately, the new owners of these properties have raised rents above what long-time residents can afford and they have been forced to move. Fewer children attend Ida B. Wells and the threat of closing the school is very real. Economic policies have not only left behind high concentrations of poverty alongside pockets of wealth, but they have a powerful effect on decisions about schools, children, and families as well.

Fullilove (2004) has underscored the effects of a changing political economy on low-income African American families, which had over generations developed close-knit communities like the one around Ida B. Wells. The role of the church was key, particularly the traditions imported from the South, and served as a kind of bulwark against oppression. They sponsored youth organizations, provided sustenance, cared for the elderly and infirm, and became an arm for political activism and education. In such contexts, both adults and institutions provided children with a sense of belonging, support, and a "reasonable" vision of future "possibilities" (Comer, 2004, p. 80). Kinship, faith, and family provided sufficient networks of support. Schools, too, anchored neighborhoods and provided a source of stability and civic engagement. It would be a mistake to romanticize the nature of the communities that grew up in response to discrimination, but it is important to understand the ways that a changing political economy has scattered families and destroyed the collective capacity that people have to solve problems.

With this kind of reality in mind, I question the public's commitment to supporting low-income families and ensuring that children and families have access to what Weiss and her colleagues describe as "critically important learning opportunities" (Weiss et al., 2009, p. 6). They suggest that policy can, and should, provide multiple pathways to help children flourish. In their meta-analysis and review of relevant research, they found that the effects of social and educational programs were most pronounced when these programs were frequent and sustained over time. To be effective, parents' involvement also has to be a shared, meaningful responsibility among multiple stakeholders.

Importantly, policies need to support and enable families to build on and leverage their assets in order to support children's learning. This involves meeting families' basic needs, including housing, nutrition, and employment, by ensuring a minimal standard of living (e.g., Rothstein, 2004). Children also need access to other types of resources such as early childhood programs, summer enrichment, and out-of-school experiences to develop 21st-century skills and intellectual competence (Weiss et al., 2009). Although questions remain about schools' commitment to what may be construed as "non-school" issues, research demonstrates that "educators . . . can indeed help address non-school-related barriers to learning, especially when they leverage human and social capital resources in support of families and other community-serving organizations and institutions" (Lawson & Alameda-Lawson, 2012, p. 679; see also Noguera, 2001; Stone, Henig, Jones, & Pierannunzi, 2001; Warren et al., 2009).

CLOSING SUGGESTIONS

In closing, I offer some "aha" moments that occurred to me as I listened to parents, children, and teachers. These moments forced me to reflect on my assumptions about parent involvement. As Compton-Lilly (2009) pointed out, these are moments that invite all of us to reconsider what we can learn in our research and our teaching. What I have learned is part of a collective narrative that illustrates the ways in which parents are invested in their children's literate lives and what matters is the nature of parents' engagement:

- All parents possess wealth and the capacity to teach valuable lessons to prepare their children for the challenges they will face in their day-to-day lives at home, at school, and in the community. By understanding and validating families' experiences, teachers can be in a better position to develop innovative strategies of instruction by connecting home and school. This means seeing differences in language and culture as potential assets on which educators can build.
- Parents' choice to be involved and how they can be involved in their children's education often rests on what they believe their children need and on their children's invitations to help them meet the challenges of school, support their interests, and reassure them in moments of self-doubt.
- Parents serve as significant role models who convey the intrinsic value of education within the context of family, faith, and community. That is, parent involvement is not always direct, but parents' own commitments, values, and actions can influence what their children believe about the value and purpose of education in the broadest sense of the word.
- Parents often approach school as the basis for their children's success and do so with a sense of urgency, whether or not their own experiences in school were positive.
- Children make visible the reciprocal, caring relationships between children and their families that often go unnoticed in studies of parent involvement. Importantly, how children act on their

parents' support depends on children's own sense of learning readiness, motivation, and self-efficacy.

- Children help us see the extent to which parents are often part of a larger support system for children who also rely on teachers, peers, mentors, tutors, and others to make decisions and develop a sense of well-being. Parents can be in the foreground at times and in the background at others. Children's stories bring into focus the value of having a wide network of support as a means to flourish.
- Children's stories about learning tell us about the different ways their parents animate their interest in learning. This was particularly true when parents motivated them to look up information on their own to find out about the subjects that interested them most. In turn, children challenge the premise underlying many calls for increased parent involvement— that parents should simply support the status quo in school, where learning and teaching have become increasingly more structured as a result of reforms that call for more testing and accountability.

I cannot help but think about the sense of urgency with which parents expressed their hopes for the children's future. The stories that fill the pages of *Race, Community, and Urban Schools* represent a small group of parents and families whose children attend public schools like Ida B. Wells. Schools in low-income neighborhoods are under the greatest threat of surveillance in a system that has embraced increased standardization, regimentation, and testing. These are schools that already lack resources and that will suffer the most from budget shortfalls at the state and local levels affected by increased privatization. Unfortunately, a real concern is that debate and discussion about education reform, the distribution of resources, and the like have become shrouded in private interests, what Fine (1993) referred to 20 years ago as a "privatized public sphere" (p. 708). However, when parents are aware of the truth of what is happening around them, they show resolve and the capacity to create positive change. Indeed, history is a witness to a framework for parental involvement that was largely based on cultural and community values, a shared sense of responsibility, and a strong desire for social and academic excellence for African American children. The stories from the past can indeed inspire creative change borne of struggle for equity in a system, which through privatization offers a promise of quality education for the few over the many.

In closing, then, I offer the following road map for opening up spaces of hope for families at home, at school, and in the community.

- Create effective home-school relationships with a model of conversation based on reciprocity, a profound sense of empathy, and mutual understanding. Such a model can enhance collaboration and cooperation because it is based on a two-way flow of information. Parents need to know what is going on in school (e.g., classroom events, field trips, curriculum), and teachers need to know about a family's needs, interests, histories, and events. Particularly important is a teacher's ability to incorporate what he or she learns into the curriculum to connect children to learning. Children's sense of place could be a part of such a curriculum—its history, the economics of change, and the like.
- Design programs to ensure that parents have an equal voice with teachers and administrators in developing parent involvement plans. Let parents conduct focus groups and interviews to understand what parents need to support learning in the broadest sense of the word. Programs should build on and respect parents' priorities, beliefs, and values.
- Provide opportunities for critical reflection, so that parents can identify problems and raise their awareness about the strengths and assets they possess to create change.
- Focus on developing capacity and leadership among families. Families can support one another by gaining knowledge about how schools work, how to communicate with teachers, and how to obtain resources. Contrary to traditional conceptions of parent involvement, in which schools often determine the structure and content of parent activities, parents can play an active role in determining and leading programmatic initiatives. As educators, we can enhance parents' capacity to be partners and leaders in local communities and schools. We can also help increase parents' political influence as a means for transforming inequality and promoting social justice in schools.
- Create space for teachers and parents to develop learning communities in order to examine what parents and teachers believe. These learning communities could be the source of discussion about vital issues and problems. For example, inquiry groups could explore the uses of language that reaffirm deficit perspectives and that serve as an impediment to creating partnerships based on mutual respect and understanding. These groups could serve as spaces where teachers and parents can discuss and critique institutional structures in schools and the community that reproduce inequality. Together, parents and

teachers can map out the opportunity structure in neighborhoods, create networks of support, and build social and cultural capital.

- Place concepts of community, trust, and cooperation at the center of coalitions that bring diverse stakeholders together to leverage power and self-interest to create change. Successful literacy and voter registration campaigns during the Civil Rights Movement demonstrated that people not only had power "over" but the "power to . . . " do something positive. Community organizing and strategies for collaboration have the potential to create policies that include families as agents who have the power to act in the best interests of their children.

- Employ theories and conceptual frameworks such as Critical Race Theory and Critical Geography to understand the ways in which parent-school-community relationships are embedded in the racial, political, and cultural landscape of economic policy and history. Counternarratives tell us a great deal about identity and place, but we can also make visible the community cultural wealth that has emerged as a response to the corrosive effects of discrimination and the erosion of public spaces. CRT offers a historical perspective that brings into focus the ways in which African American families have long used organizing strategies to create institutions of learning as sources of hope. That history serves as the basis for challenging a dominant narrative that protects privilege and power and offers a model of political and civil action.

- Develop programs in schools that are not limited to academic concerns. Programs at schools can provide resources designed to promote economic stability, good health, and continuing education to emphasize lifelong learning, relationships, and civic engagement in order to maintain a strong sense of community. The goal of such programs can help create spaces of hope where children and families can flourish.

Community-Based Research

Much of the research I describe throughout this book, especially in Chapters 2, 3, and 4, grew out of a coalition of educators that formed the "education collaborative." This coalition included principals from local public schools, the director of the community center, and faculty in economics, psychology, and education. Faculty in the Center for Social Concerns also played a vital role in sustaining the coalition's work. In forming this coalition, we made two key assumptions: (a) goals cannot be reached by any one individual or group working alone, and (b) participants should include a *diversity* of individuals and groups who represent the concern and/or geographic area or population.

Faculty and staff at the Center for Social Concerns and the Community Learning Center respectively brought together three converging initiatives that made a coalition possible: (a) the center's focus on developing community-based research projects that would be participatory and have a long-term impact on the community; (b) the center's education programs for children in local schools and efforts to collaborate with educators in the local school district; and (c) the research that undergraduates were conducting at area public schools through a senior seminar they were taking to complete a minor in education.

Our initial efforts were focused on discussing community-based research as a participatory approach to (a) identifying relevant problems, (b) developing a shared vision of goals and methodologies, and (c) formulating a strategic plan for reaching those goals (Stoecker, 2005; Strand, Marullo, Cutforth, Stoecker, & Donohue, 2003). Such an approach served more as a heuristic than a linear approach to research. This means that we knew we needed to touch on each of these components, but with the understanding that our conceptions at any stage could change. After all, much research begins with identifying a problem, reading about how others have defined a similar problem, and then returning to refine the problem. This was especially true of our efforts to think strategically about possible impacts. We agreed that we needed to remain flexible in addressing issues surrounding the Black-White achievement education gap in schools, the dropout rate, safety, parent engagement, and teacher quality.

Discussions centered on defining issues and creating priorities among the many issues that the group felt we could address immediately given the resources we had at hand. These resources included both the time and relevant expertise necessary to develop systematic efforts to do research that would have a long-term impact. This also meant reaching a shared understanding of problems and vision through much give-and-take and negotiation among different stakeholders.

Importantly, each of the meetings of the education collaborative was held at a different site to emphasize shared leadership and ownership. Two of the principals hosted meetings that included dinner and essentially "chaired" meetings. Faculty and staff also hosted dinners at their homes, shared resources, and initiated conversations about critical issues. The result of changing the locus of power and leadership was very much in keeping with models of a participatory democracy. In fact, neither power nor leadership were univocal as much as they were relational. At times, people took on the role of expert and teacher, while at other times these roles would be reversed: teachers and experts became students. The respect that we showed one another contributed to developing trusting relationships. In addition, individual members' commitments to equity and change enabled us to put aside self-interest about what issues to pursue first and how to do so.

The education collaborative had the support of educators, the community, and a research university, which provided necessary resources to create the conditions for both action and change. In the end, we were able to (a) accomplish meaningful tasks collectively; (b) build capacity among members of the group, rather than having different groups compete for power (Warren, 2005); and (c) ensure that power was accompanied by both trust and collaboration.

Interviews of Teachers in Chapter 1

Interviews were conducted with the principal of Ida B. Wells, one additional administrator, and nine teachers who taught the children of parents who were participating in parent meetings. Of the 11 educators, 6 were White females and the administrator was a White male. The principal and three female teachers were African American. Their overall average experience was 16 years and all held a master's degree.

Interviews were conducted in teachers' own classrooms for approximately 1 hour and focused on teachers' understanding of what parent involvement means, their experiences with parent-teacher conferences, the ways they reached out to parents, the factors that teachers believed fostered increased parent involvement, and those factors that may have challenged parents' involvement at home or at school. All interviews were transcribed and analyzed in order to address the overarching questions motivating the study of parent involvement (Greene & Long, 2010), namely, how do teachers define parent involvement and what are the conditions that might foster increased involvement? I read each transcript, wrote a narrative based on each educator's response, identified themes that were similar and different across the transcripts, and culled the transcripts for illustrations.

Research Methodology for Chapter 2

In-depth interviews were conducted with each of the parents 2 weeks before parent meetings were scheduled to begin. Each interview lasted up to 45 minutes and helped to document parents' life histories. The script of questions, based on Fine and Weis's (1998) study of adults living in poverty, prompted parents to reflect on their own experiences at school, their parents' education and involvement in their education, the neighborhoods where they grew up, and their lives now as parents, including their working lives, neighborhoods, and relationships with their children. These interviews were recorded by video camera and audiotaped in a classroom at the school.

Each of the parents also participated in a focus group a week before the parents began to attend parent meetings. It was held at two different times in order to accommodate work schedules. These focus groups provided a supportive environment for parents to describe the ways in which they were involved in their children's education, as well as the challenges they faced. Parents' stories also served as a springboard for discussions in parent meetings.

Finally, informal conversations with each parent, recorded in field notes, strengthened the portrait of parent involvement that evolved over a 2-year period. These conversations took place at school and in other settings, such as the library and a local museum that parents visited with their children as part of the workshops or over meals that preceded weekly meetings.

All data were transcribed and analyzed to address the central questions motivating the study: How did parents see their role in their children's education and to what extent did the parents' views change over time? I parsed interview and focus-group transcripts into t-units, which consist of independent clauses and any embedded subordinate clauses. By coding transcripts at a syntactic level of meaning, I sought to account for more of the data in the interviews and focus groups than researchers typically analyze. (See Greene, 2013, for more information about this approach to coding the transcripts.)

I took a grounded theory (Glaser & Strauss, 1967) approach to interpreting the transcripts. I then identified the categories of parent roles as an "evolving and iterative process" (Barton et al., 2004). More specifically, I read all of the transcripts, wrote narratives that captured the individual differences among the parents' life histories and approaches to parent involvement, and then merged my analyses to develop categories. The typology of parent roles that Auerbach (2007) developed also served as a guide for my analysis. These roles ranged from moral and emotional supporter to supporter and advocate. Auerbach characterized parents' strategies as existing along a continuum from passive (e.g., indirect, behind the scenes, hands-off) to proactive (e.g., direct, instrumental, hands-on). For Auerbach (2007), advocacy (i.e., "struggling advocates") was a proactive role that was more often than not connected to parents' presence at school (for more detail, see Greene, 2013).

Family Profiles

Name	Age	Gender	Race	Education Completed	Number of Children
Keisha	51	F	African American	Middle School	4
Amy	36	F	Mixed Race	High School	7
Albert	32	M	Hispanic	Middle School	2
Carol	39	F	African American	BA	4
Marc	32	M	African American	High School	7
Latrisse	29	F	African American	High School	3
Beatrice	37	F	African American	GED	7
Maya	26	F	African American	Middle School	4
Lamont	47	M	African American	High School	2
Paviel	34	F	African American	GED	5
Devon	52	M	African American	High School	2
Therese	26	F	African American	Middle School	6
Richard	29	M	African American	GED	6
Damian	45	M	African American	High School	5
Dionna	31	F	African American	High School	3
Milo	31	M	African American	High School	3
Mary	53	F	Caucasian	High School	2

Research Methodology for Chapter 3

The four case examples were drawn from a larger pool of 26 children who participated in a 3-year longitudinal study. In the cases I develop, I have sought to illustrate the ways that children described their parents' involvement, how their parents' strategies changed over time, and some of the challenges both parents and children faced in different contexts. The racial and socioeconomic backgrounds of these four cases represent the larger pool from which they were drawn. However, they are not altogether representative of all children who participated in this study.

All of the children were initially enrolled as 3rd and 4th graders in ten Title 1 primary schools. All of these schools were in various stages of corrective action because their students' performance on high-stakes tests had not met federal standards. Altogether there were 17 girls and 9 boys. Fourteen of the children identified themselves as African American, 1 as Asian, 6 as Latino/a, 1 as mixed race, and 4 as European American. All of the children reported on a survey that they were on paid or reduced lunch.

The 26 children are those children who remained in the school district after 3 years and from whom we have collected interviews for all 3 years of the study. Working with the director of the school district's parent involvement coordinator and the director of research in Year 1, I was able to interview 98 children whose parents participated in a parent involvement program designed to foster increased home literacy (e.g., reading with children, helping children study, and accompanying children to the library), school readiness (e.g., motivating children to want to learn), and parents' presence at school.

A researcher met with the children once a year for an hour to conduct what might be described as semistructured interviews in a room designated by the Parent Support Specialist at the children's school. This meant that the questions were scripted, but we routinely asked follow-up questions to prompt children to elaborate, share related information, and introduce relevant issues. Questions focused on children's daily routine before, during, and after school; who they studied and did their homework with;

whether or not they read with their parents; the extent to which they were involved in extracurricular activities; whether or not they had opportunities to go to the zoo, the park, or cultural events; conversations they had with their parents about the news; and discussions they may have had about their future goals.

Each interview was transcribed completely, and I read children's stories looking for both individual differences and recurring themes in each of the interviews to understand the roles their parents played in their education. In Year 3, I wrote narratives about each of the remaining 26 students and included extended examples of parents and children reading together, going to the library, studying, doing homework, spending time with friends, and the like. As in Compton-Lilly's study (2009), I then compared cases, developed a set of categories, and merged analyses of each family to develop a portrait of parent involvement without losing the nuance of individual families. As I read the nuanced stories of individual children, I also began to hear a collective story (Lawrence-Lightfoot, 2003) of children's experiences at home, in school, and in the community.

References

Alexander, K. (2013). Asymmetric information, parental choice, vouchers, charter schools and Stiglitz. Available at http://horacemannleague.blogspot.com/2013/01/asymmetric-information-parental-choice.html?m=1

Allen, J. (2007). *Creating welcoming schools: A practical guide to home-school partnerships with diverse families.* New York: Teachers College Press.

Allen, J. (2010). *Literacy in the welcoming classroom: Creating family-school partnerships that support student learning.* New York: Teachers College Press.

Anderson, J. (1988). *The education of Blacks in the South, 1860–1935.* Chapel Hill: The University of North Carolina Press.

Anyon, J. (2005). *Radical possibilities: Public policy, urban education, and a new social movement.* London: Routledge.

Anzaldua, G. (2007). *Borderlands/La Frontera* (3rd ed.). San Francisco: Aunt Lute Books.

Apple, M. (2006). *Educating the "right" way: Markets, standards, God, and inequality* (2nd ed.). New York: Routledge.

Apple, M. (2011). Policy for the poor and poor education policy: An essay review of *Education and poverty in affluent countries. Education Review, 14*(10). Available at http://www.edrev.info/essay/v14n10.pdf

Archambault, R. D. (Ed.). (1964). *John Dewey on education: Selected writings.* New York: Random House.

Auerbach, S. (2001). "Why do they give the good classes to some and not to others?" Latino parent narratives of struggle in a college access program. *Teachers College Record, 104*(7), 1369–1392.

Auerbach, S. (2007). From moral supporters to struggling advocates: Reconceptualizing parent roles in education through the experience of working-class families of color. *Urban Education, 42*(3), 250–283.

Auerbach, S. (Ed.). (2011). *School leadership for authentic family and community partnerships: Research perspectives for transforming practice.* New York: Routledge.

Barge, J., & Loges, W. (2003). Parent, student, and teacher perceptions of parental involvement. *Journal of Applied Communication Research, 31*(2), 140–163.

Barton, A. C., Drake, C., Perez, J. G., St. Louis, K., & George, M. (2004). Ecologies of parental engagement in urban education. *Educational Researcher, 33*(4), 3–12.

Berliner, D. (2014). Effects of inequality and poverty vs. teachers and schooling on America's youth. *Teachers College Record.* Available at http:www.tcrecord.org/PrintContent.asp?ContentID=16889

Bourdieu, P. (1993). *The field of cultural production: Essays on art and literature* (J. Randal, Ed.). New York: Columbia University Press.

Brandt, D. (2001). *Literacy in American lives.* New York: Cambridge University Press.

Bronfenbrenner, U. (1994). Ecological models of human development. In T. Postlethwaite & T. Husen (Eds.), *International encyclopedia of education* (2nd ed., pp. 1643–1647). Oxford, UK: Elsevier.

Brooks, D. (2013). When families fail. Available at http://www.nytimes.com/2013/02/15/opinion/brooks-crayons-to-college.html?emc=eta1

Buendia, E., Ares, N., Juarez, B. G., & Peercy, M. (2004). The geographies of difference: The production of the east side, west side, and central side school. *American Educational Research Journal, 41*(4), 833–863.

Cecelski, D. (1994). *Along freedom road: Hyde county, North Carolina, and the fate of Black schools in the south.* Charlotte: University of North Carolina Press.

Chilcot, L. (Producer), & Guggenheim, D. (Director). (2010). *Waiting for Superman.* United States: Participant Media.

Children's Defense Fund. (2011). *Portrait of inequality: Black children in America.* Washington, DC: Children's Defense Fund.

Clark, R. M. (1983). *Family life and school achievement: Why poor Black children succeed or fail.* Chicago: The University of Chicago Press.

Coleman, J., Campbell, E., Hobson, C., McPartland, J., Mood, A., Weinfeld, F., & York, T. (1966). *Equality of educational opportunity (The Coleman Report).* Washington, DC: U.S. Government Printing Office.

Comer, J. (2004). *Leave no child behind: Preparing today's youth for tomorrow's world.* New Haven, CT: Yale University Press.

Compton-Lilly, C. (2003). *Reading families: The literate lives of urban children.* New York: Teachers College Press.

Compton-Lilly, C. (2007). *Re-reading families: The literate lives of urban children: Four years later.* New York: Teachers College Press.

Compton-Lilly, C. (2009). Listening to families over time: Seven lessons learned about literacy in families. *Language Arts, 86*(6), 449–457.

Compton-Lilly, C. (2012). *Reading time: The literate lives of urban secondary students and their families.* New York: Teachers College Press.

Compton-Lilly, C., & Greene, S. (Eds.). (2010). *Bedtime stories and book reports: Connecting parent involvement and family literacy.* New York: Teachers College Press.

Cooper, E. J. (2008). Realities and responsibilities in the education villages. In L. Tillman (Ed.), *The SAGE handbook of African American education* (pp. 435–449). Thousand Oaks, CA: Sage.

Coordinating Committee of the Community Forum for Economic Development. (2012). Projects of the community forum. Report to the Membership, St. Joseph County, IN.

Crenshaw, K. (2011). Twenty years of Critical Race Theory: Looking back to move forward. Available at http://connecticutlawreview.org/articles/twenty-years-of-critical-race-theory-looking-back-to-move-forward/

Cresswell, T. (2004). *Place: A short introduction.* Malden, MA: Blackwell Publishing.

Cucchiara, M. (2008). Re-branding urban schools: Urban revitalization, social status, and marketing public schools to the upper middle class. *Journal of Education Policy, 23*(2), 165–179.

Cucchiara, M. B., & Horvat, E. M. (2009). Perils and promises: Middle-class parental involvement in urban schools. *American Educational Research Journal, 46*(4), 974–1004.

Darling-Hammond, L. (2010). *The flat world and education: How America's commitment to equality will determine our future.* New York: Teachers College Press.

Delgado Bernal, D. (1998). Using a Chicana feminist epistemology in education research. *Harvard Education Review, 68*(4), 555–582.

Delgado Bernal, D. (2002). Critical race theory, Latino critical theory, and critical raced-gendered epistemologies: Recognizing students of color as holders and creators of knowledge. *Qualitative Inquiry.* Available at http://newsletter.ed.utah.edu/ELP/CourseMaterials/Aleman_7960/DelgadoBernal-02

Delpit, L. (2012). *Multiplication is for White people: Raising our expectations for other people's children.* New York: The New Press.

Deslandes, R., & Cloutier, R. (2002). Adolescents' perceptions of parent involvement in schooling. *School Psychology International, 23,* 220–232.

Division of Community Development and Civic Alliance. (2005). *South Bend City Plan.* South Bend, IN: Division of Community Development and Civic Alliance.

DuBois, W. E. B. (2009). *The souls of Black folk.* New York: Library of America.

Dudley-Marling, C. (2009). Home-school literacy connections: The perceptions of African American and immigrant ESL parents in two urban communities. *Teachers College Record, 111*(7), 1713–1752.

Edelman, M. W. (2012). America's public schools: Still unequal and unjust. Available at http://www.huffingtonpost.com/marian-wright-edelman/public-schools-minority-students_b_1408878.html

Edwards, P. (1993). Before and after school desegregation: African-American parent involvement in schools. *Educational Policy: An Interdisciplinary Journal of Policy and Practice, 7*(3), 340–369.

Edwards, P., McMillon, G., & Turner, J. (2010). *Change is gonna come: Transforming literacy education for African American students.* New York: Teachers College Press.

Englund, M., Luckner, A., Whaley, G., & Egeland, B. (2004). Children's achievement in early elementary school: Longitudinal effects of parental involvement, expectations, and quality of assistance. *Journal of Educational Psychology, 96*(4), 723–730.

Epps, E. G. (1983). Foreword. In R. M. Clark (Ed.), *Family life and school achievement: Why poor Black children succeed or fail* (pp. ix–xiii). Chicago: University of Chicago Press.

Epstein, J. L. (1995). School/family/community partnerships: Caring for the children we share. *Phi Delta Kappan, 76*(9), 701–712.

Epstein, J. L. (2010). *School, family, and community partnerships: Preparing educators and improving schools* (2nd ed.). New York: Westview Press.

Feagin, J. F. (1998). *The new urban paradigm: Critical perspectives on the city.* Lanham, MD: Rowman & Littlefield.

Ferguson, A. (2001). *Bad boys: Public schools in the making of Black masculinity.* Ann Arbor, MI: University of Michigan Press.

Fessler, P. (2011). Making it in the U.S.: More than just hard work. Available at www.npr./2011/09/15/140428359/making-it-in-the-u-s-more-than-just-hard-work

Fine, M. (1993). [Ap]parent involvement: Reflections on parents, power, and urban public schools. *Teachers College Record, 94*(4), 681–728.

Fine, M., & Weis, L. (1998). *The unknown city: The lives of poor and working-class young adults.* Boston: Beacon Press.

Fisher, M. T. (2009). *Black literate lives: Historical and contemporary perspectives.* New York: Routledge.

Freire, P. (1970). *Pedagogy of the oppressed.* New York: Continuum.

Freire, P. (1974). *Education for critical consciousness.* New York: Continuum.

Fullilove, M. T. (2004). *Root shock: How tearing up city neighborhoods hurts America, and what we can do about it.* New York: Ballantine Books.

Furstenberg, F. F., Cook, T. D., Eccles, J., Elder, G. H., & Sameroff, A. (1999). *Managing to make it: Urban families and adolescent success.* Chicago: University of Chicago Press.

Gadsden, V. L. (1993). Literacy, education, and identity among African-Americans: The communal nature of learning. *Urban Education, 27*(4), 352–369.

Gadsden, V. (1996). Designing and conducting family literacy programs that account for racial, ethnic, religious, and other cultural differences. In L. A. Benjamin & J. Lord (Eds.), *Family literacy: Directions in research and implications for practice* (pp. 248–267). Washington, DC: Pelavin Research Institute.

Giroux, H. (1987). Literacy and the pedagogy of political empowerment. In P. Freire & D. Macedo (Eds.), *Literacy: Reading the word and the world* (pp. 1–27). London: Routledge.

Glaser, B., & Strauss, A. (1967). *The discovery of grounded theory: Strategies for qualitative research.* Chicago: Aldine Press.

Goldring, E., Cohen-Vogel, L., Smrekar, C., & Taylor, C. (2006). Schooling closer to home: Desegregation policy and neighborhood contexts. *American Journal of Education, 112*(3), 335–362.

Grant, C. (2012). Cultivating flourishing lives: A robust social justice vision of education. *American Educational Research Association, 49*(5), 910–934.

Graue, E. (1999). Representing relationships between parents and schools: Making visible the force of theory. *Parenthood in America,* 1–13. Available at http://parenthood.library.wisc.edu/Graue/Graue.html

Graue, E., & Hawkins, M. (2010). "I always feel they don't know anything about us": Diverse families talk about their relations with school. In M. Marsh & T. Turner-Vorbeck (Eds.), *(Mis)Understanding families: Learning from real families in our schools* (pp. 109–125). New York: Teachers College Press.

Greene, S. (2001). Argument as conversation: The role of inquiry in writing a researched argument. In W. Bishop & P. Zemliansky (Eds.), *The subject is research* (pp. 145–164). Portsmouth, NH: Boynton/Cook Heinemann.

Greene, S. (2008). (Ed.). *Literacy as a civil right: Reclaiming social justice in literacy teaching and learning.* New York: Peter Lang Publishing.

Greene, S. (2013). Mapping low-income African American parents' roles in their children's education in a changing political economy. *Teachers College Record, 115*(10). Available at www.tcrecord.org, ID number 17155.

Greene, S., & Abt-Perkins, D. (2003). (Eds.). *Making race visible: Literacy research for cultural understanding.* New York: Teachers College Press.

Greene, S., Burke, K., & McKenna, M. (2013). Forms of voice: Exploring the empowerment of youth at the intersection of art and action. *The Urban Review, 45*(3), 311–334.

Greene, S., Burke, K., & McKenna, M. (in press). Re-framing spatial inequality: Youth, photography and a changing urban landscape. In H. R. Hall & C. Cole-Robinson (Eds.), *Shifting demographics: A cross-disciplinary look at race and class in 21st century America.* New York: Peter Lang.

Greene, S., & Lidinsky, A. (2011). *From inquiry to academic writing: A practical guide* (2nd ed.). Boston: Bedford Books.

Greene, S., & Long, J. (2010). Flipping the script: Honoring and supporting parent involvement. In C. Compton-Lilly & S. Greene (Eds.), *Bedtime stories and book reports: Connecting parent involvement and family literacy* (pp. 15–26). New York: Teachers College Press.

Grolnick, W. S., Ryan, R. M., & Deci, E. L. (1991). Inner resources for school achievement: Motivational mediators of children's perceptions of their parents. *Journal of Educational Psychology, 83*(4), 508–517.

Grolnick, W. S., & Slowiaczek, M. L. (1994). Parents' involvement in children's schooling: A multidimensional conceptualization and motivational model. *Child Development, 65*(1), 237–252.

Gutiérrez, K. D. (2008). Language and literacies as civil rights. In S. Greene (Ed.), *Literacy as a civil right: Reclaiming social justice in literacy teaching and learning* (pp. 169–184). New York: Peter Lang Publishing.

Gutiérrez, K. D. (2011). Teaching toward possibility: Building cultural supports for robust learning. *Powerplay: A Journal of Educational Justice, 3*(1), 22–37.

Gutiérrez, K. D., & Rogoff, B. (2003). Cultural ways of learning: Individual traits or repertoires of practice. *Educational Researcher, 32*(5), 19–25.

Hacker, J., & Pierson, P. (2010). *Winner-take-all politics: How Washington made the rich richer—and turned its back on the middle class.* New York: Simon & Schuster.

Hall, H. R., & Cole-Robinson, C. (Eds.). (in press). *Shifting demographics: A cross-disciplinary look at race and class in 21st century America.* New York: Peter Lang Publishing.

Harris, D. (2006). Race, class, and privacy in the ordinary postwar house, 1945–1950. In R. Schein (Ed.), *Landscape and race in the United States* (pp. 127–155). New York: Routledge.

Hart, B., & Risley, T. (1995). *Meaningful differences in the everyday experience of young American children.* Baltimore, MD: Paul H. Brookes.

Harvey, D. (2007). *A brief history of neoliberalism.* New York: Oxford University Press.

Harvey, D. (2009). *Social justice and the city* (revised ed.). Athens: The University of Georgia Press.

Haymes, S. (1995). *Race, culture, and the city: A pedagogy for Black urban struggle.* Albany: State University of New York Press.

Heath, S. B. (1983). *Ways with words: Language, life and work in communities and classrooms.* Cambridge, UK: Cambridge University Press.

Henderson, A. T., & Mapp, K. L. (2002). *A new wave of evidence: The impact of school, family, and community connections on student achievement.* Austin, TX: Southwest Educational Development Laboratory.

Hollander, C. (2012, April 22). Teach the books, teach the heart. *New York Times.* Available at http://www.nytimes.com/2012/04/22/opinion/sunday/taking-emotions-out-of-our-schools.html?pagewanted=all&_r=0

Hoover-Dempsey, K., & Sandler, H. (1995). Parental involvement in children's education: Why does it make a difference? *Teachers College Record, 97*(2), 310–331.

Hoover-Dempsey, K. V., Walker, J. M., Sandler, H. M., Whetsel, D., Green, C. L., & Wilkins, A. S. (2005). Why do parents become involved? Research findings and implications. *The Elementary School Journal, 106*(2), 105–130.

Horvat, E. M., Weininger, E. B., & Lareau, A. (2003). From social ties to social capital: Class differences in the relations between schools and parent networks. *American Educational Research Journal, 67*(1), 319–352.

Howard, T. C. (2010). *Why race and culture matter in schools: Closing the achievement gap in America's classrooms.* New York: Teachers College Press.

Irvine, R., & Irvine, J. (1983). The impact of the desegregation process on the education of Black students: Key variables. *Journal of Negro Education, 52*(4), 410–422.

Jackson, J. (1983, March). *Parents must help their children in school.* Speech presented at Operation Push, Chicago.

Jeynes, W. (2005). A meta-analysis of the relation of parent involvement to urban elementary school student academic achievement. *Urban Education, 40*(3), 237–269.

Katz, M. B. (2001). *The price of citizenship: Redefining the American welfare state*. New York: Owl Books.

Kilbride, K. (2012, August 19). Too many waivers? South Bend numbers above state average. *South Bend Tribune*. Available at http://www.southbendtribune .com/news/sbt-20120819sbtmicha-01-02-20120819,0,767723.story

Kinloch, V. (2010). *Harlem on our minds: Place, race, and the literacies of urban youth*. New York: Teachers College Press.

Kinloch, V. (2012). *Crossing boundaries: Teaching and learning with urban youth*. New York: Teachers College Press.

Kochhar, R., Fry, R., & Taylor. P. (2011). Wealth gaps rise to record highs between Whites, Blacks, Hispanics. Available at http://www.pewsocialtrends.org/2011 /07/26/wealth-gaps-rise-to-record-highs-between-whites-blacks-hispanics/

Kohn, A. (2013). Is parent involvement in school really useful? Available at http://www.washingtonpost.com/blogs/answer-sheet/wp/2013/02/06 /is-parent-involvement-in-school-really-useful/

Kozol, J. (1967). *Death at an early age: The destruction of the hearts and minds of Negro children in the Boston Public Schools*. Boston: Houghton Mifflin.

Kozol, J. (2005). Still separate, still unequal: America's educational apartheid. *Harper's Magazine, 311*, 1–25. Available at http://www.mindfully.org/Reform/2005/ American-Apartheid-Education1sep05.htm

Ladson-Billings, G. (2003). Foreword. In S. Greene & D. Abt-Perkins (Eds.), *Making race visible: Literacy research for cultural understanding* (pp. vii–xi). New York: Teachers College Press.

Ladson-Billings, G. (2006). From the achievement gap to the education debt: Understanding achievement in U.S. schools. *Educational Researcher, 35*(7), 3–12.

Ladson-Billings, G., & Tate, W. (1995). Toward a critical race theory of education. *Teachers College Record, 97*(1), 47–68.

Lareau, A. (2000). *Home advantage: Social class and parental intervention*. New York: Rowman & Littlefield Publishers.

Lareau, A. (2003). *Unequal childhoods: Class, race, and family life*. Berkeley: University of California Press.

Lareau, A., & Horvat, E. (1999). Moments of social inclusion: Race, class and culture. *Sociology of Education, 71*(1), 39–56.

Lawrence-Lightfoot, S. (2003). *The essential conversation: What parents and teachers can learn from each other*. New York: Ballantine Books.

Lawson, M., & Alameda-Lawson, T. (2012). A case study of school-linked, collective parent engagement. *American Educational Research Journal, 49*(4), 651–684.

Lee, S. J., & Bowen, N. (2006). Parent involvement, cultural capital, and the achievement gap among elementary school children. *American Educational Research Journal, 43*(2), 193–218.

Lewis, A. E. (2003). *Race in the schoolyard: Negotiating the color line in classrooms and communities*. New Brunswick, NJ: Rutgers University Press.

Lewis, A. E. (2008). "Even sweet, gentle Larry?" The continuing significance of race. In S. Greene (Ed.), *Literacy as a civil right: Reclaiming social justice in literacy teaching and learning* (pp. 69–86). New York: Peter Lang Publishing.

Li, G. (2010). Social class, culture, and "good parenting": Voices of low-SES families. In M. Marsh & T. Turner-Vorbeck (Eds.), *(Mis)understanding families: Learning from real families in our schools* (pp. 162–178). New York: Teachers College Press.

Lipman, P. (2004). *High stakes education: Inequality, globalization, and urban school reform.* New York: RoutledgeFalmer.

Lipman, P. (2008). Education policy, race, and neoliberal urbanism. In S. Greene (Ed.), *Literacy as a civil right: Reclaiming social justice in literacy teaching and learning* (pp. 45–66). New York: Peter Lang.

Lipman, P. (2011). *The new political economy of urban education: Neoliberalism, race, and the right to the city.* New York: Routledge.

Long, J. (2010). Transformative change: Parent involvement as a process of identity development. In C. Compton-Lilly & S. Greene (Eds.), *Bedtime stories and book reports: Connecting parent involvement and family literacy* (pp. 40–51). New York: Teachers College Press.

Lopez, G., & Parker, L. (Eds.). (2003). *Interrogating racism in qualitative research methodology.* New York: Peter Lang Publishing.

Marty, M. (2005). *When faiths collide.* London: Blackwell.

Massey, D. S., & Denton, N. A. (1993). *American apartheid: Segregation and the making of the underclass.* Cambridge, MA: Harvard University Press.

Matsuda, M. J., Lawrence, C. R., Delgado, R., & Crenshaw, K. W. (1993). *Words that wound: Critical race theory, assaultive speech, and the First Amendment.* Boulder, CO: Westview Press.

McHenry, E. (2002). *Forgotten readers: Recovering the lost history of African American literary societies.* Durham, NC: Duke University Press.

Miller, P. (2011). Mapping educational opportunity zones: A geospatial analysis of neighborhood block groups. *Urban Review, 44*(2), 189–218.

Moll, L. C. (2005). Reflections and possibilities. In N. Gonzalez, L. Moll, & C. Amanti (Eds.), *Funds of knowledge: Theorizing practice in households, communities and classrooms* (pp. 275–288). Mahwah, NJ: Erlbaum.

Murray, C. (2009). Youth parent and teacher relationships as predictors of school engagement and functioning among low-income urban youth. *The Journal of Early Adolescence, 29*(3), 376–404.

National Commission on Excellence in Education. (1983). *A nation at risk: The imperative for educational reform.* Washington, DC: U.S. Government Printing Office.

Nespor, J. (1997). *Tangled up in school: Politics, space, bodies, and signs in the educational process.* Mahwah, NJ: Lawrence Erlbaum Associates.

Neuman, S. B., & Celano, D. (2001). Access to print in low-income and middle-income communities: An ecological study of four neighbornhoods. *Reading Research Quarterly, 36*(1), 8–26.

Noguera, P. (2001). Transforming urban schools through investments in the social capital of parents. In S. Saegert, J. Thompson, & M. Warren (Eds.), *Social capital and poor communities* (pp. 189–212). New York: Russell Sage Foundation.

Norton, N. (2010). God's people are strong: Children's spiritual literacy practices. In C. Compton-Lilly & S. Greene (Eds.), *Bedtime stories and book reports: Connecting parent involvement and family literacy* (pp. 111–122). New York: Teachers College Press.

Nussbaum, M. (1997). *Cultivating humanity: A classical defense of reform in liberal education*. Cambridge, MA: Harvard University Press.

Oakes, J. (2005). *Keeping track: How schools structure inequality*. New Haven, CT: Yale University Press.

Oakes, J., & Guiton, G. (1995). Matchmaking: The dynamics of high school tracking decisions. *American Educational Research Journal, 32*(1), 3–34.

Obama, B. (2011, September). "Remarks by the President on No Child Left Behind." Speech presented in Washington, DC. Available at http://www.whitehouse.gov/the-press-office/2011/09/23/remarks-president-no-child-left-behind-flexibility

Ordoñez-Jasis, R., & Flores, S. (2010). *Descubriendo historias*/uncovering stories: The literacy worlds of Latino children and families. In C. Compton-Lilly & S. Greene (Eds.), *Bedtime stories and book reports: Connecting parent involvement and family* (pp. 124–137). New York: Teachers College Press.

Orfield, G. (1997). *Dismantling desegregation: The quiet reversal of Brown v. Board of Education*. New York: New Press.

Orfield, G., & Gordon, N. (Eds.). (2001). *Schools more separate: Consequences of a decade of resegregation*. Cambridge, MA: The Civil Rights Project, Harvard University.

Paige, R., & Witty, E. (2010). *The Black-White achievement gap: Why closing it is the greatest civil rights issue of our time*. Chicago: American Management Association.

Paulson, S., Marchant, G., & Rothilsberg, B. (1998). Early adolescents' perceptions of patterns of parents' achievement. *Journal of Early Adolescence, 14*(1), 250–267.

Payne, C. M. (2008). *So much reform so little change: The persistence of failure in urban schools*. Cambridge, MA: Harvard University Press.

Perry, T., Steele, C., & Hilliard, A., III. (2003). *Young, gifted, and Black: Promoting high achievement among African American students*. Boston: Beacon Press.

Peshkin, A. (2000). The nature of interpretation in qualitative research. *Educational Researcher, 29*(9), 5–10.

Purcell-Gates, V. (1995). *Other people's words*. Boston: Harvard University Press.

Pushor, D. (2010). Are schools doing enough to learn about families? In M. Miller & T. Turner-Vorbeck (Eds.), *(Mis)understanding families: Learning from real families in our schools* (pp. 4–16). New York: Teachers College Press.

Richardson, E. (2003). *African American literacies*. New York: Routledge.

Rodríguez-Brown, F. V. (2009). *The home-schooled connection: Lessons learned in a culturally and linguistically diverse community*. New York: Routledge.

Rogers, R. (2003). *A critical discourse analysis of family literacy practices: Power in and out of print*. New York: Routledge.

Rogers, R., & O'Brien, D. (2010). Parent involvement with a purpose: Get the lead out! In C. Compton-Lilly & S. Greene (Eds.), *Bedtime stories and book reports: Connecting parent involvement and family literacy* (pp. 52–64). New York: Teachers College Press.

Rose, M. (1988). *Lives on the boundary: A moving account of the struggles and achievements of America's educationally underprepared*. New York: Penguin.

Rothstein, R. (2004). *Class and schools: Using social, economic, and educational reform to close the Black-White achievement gap*. New York: Economic Policy Institute and Teachers College Press.

Sabol, W. J., West, H. C., & Cooper, M. (2010). Prisoners in 2008. *Bureau of Justice Statistics Bulletin*. Washington, DC: U.S. Department of Justice. Available at http://bjs.ojp.usdoj.gov/content/pub/pdf/p08.pdf

Sampson, R., Morenoff, J., & Gannon-Rowley, T. (2002). "Neighborhood effects": Social processes and new directions in research. *Annual Review of Sociology, 28*, 443–478.

Sampson, W. A. (2004). *Black and brown: Race, ethnicity, and school preparation*. Lanham, MD: Scarecrow.

Sangha, S. (2013, February 24). City's parents encounter a waiting list for almost everything. *The New York Times*, p. 23.

Santow, M. (2007). Running in place: Saul Alinsky, race, and community organizing. In M. Orr (Ed.), *Transforming the city: Community organizing and the challenge of political change* (pp. 28–55). Lawrence: University Press of Kansas.

Schein, R. H. (Ed.). (2006). *Landscape and race in the United States*. New York: Routledge.

Schott Foundation for Public Education. (2010). *Yes we can: The Schott 50 state report on public education and Black males*. Cambridge, MA: Author.

Schultz, K. (2009). *Rethinking classroom participation: Listening to silent voices*. New York: Teachers College Press.

Shipler, D. K. (2005). *The working poor: Invisible in America*. New York: Vintage Books.

Smagorinsky, P. (2012). What do we care about when we care about education? Available at http://athens.patch.com/articles/what-do-we-care-about-when-we-care-about-education-94ed6deb

Smith, N. (2008). *Uneven development: Nature, capital, and the production of space* (3rd ed.). Athens: University of Georgia Press.

Soja, E. W. (2010). *Seeking spatial justice*. Minneapolis: University of Minnesota Press.

Sokolower, J. (2012). Schools and the new Jim Crow: An interview with Michelle Alexander. *Rethinking Schools*. Available at http://www.rethinkingschools.org/archive/26_02/26_02_sokolower.shtml

Solórzano, D., & Yosso, T. (2002). Critical race methodology: Counter-storytelling as an analytical framework for educational research. *Qualitative Inquiry, 8*, 23–44.

Squires, G. D., & Kubrin, C. E. (2005). Privileged places: Race, uneven development and the geography of opportunity in urban America. *Urban Studies, 42*(1), 47–68.

St. Joseph County Housing Consortium. (2005). *Housing and community development plan.* South Bend, IN: The St. Joseph County Housing Committee.

Stanton-Salazar, R. D. (1997). A social capital framework for understanding the socialization of racial minority children and youths. *Harvard Educational Review, 67*(1), 1–40.

Stewart, E. B., Stewart, E. A., & Simons, R. L. (2007). The effect of neighborhood context on the college aspirations of African American adolescents. *American Educational Research Journal, 44*(4), 896–919.

Stoecker, R. (2005). *Research methods for community change: A project-based approach.* Thousand Oaks, CA: Sage.

Stone, C., Henig, J., Jones, B., & Pierannunzi, C. (2001). *Building capacity: The politics of reforming urban schools.* Lawrence: University of Kansas Press.

Strand, K., Marullo, S., Cutforth, N., Stoecker, R., & Donohue, P. (2003). *Community-based research and higher education.* San Francisco: Jossey-Bass.

Tatum, B. (2007). *Can we talk about race? And other conversations in an era of school resegregation.* Boston: Beacon Press.

Taylor, D., & Dorsey-Gaines, C. (1988). *Growing up literate: Learning from inner city families.* Portsmouth, NH: Heinemann.

Teale, W. H. (1986). Home background and young children's literacy development. In W. H. Teale & E. Sulzby (Eds.), *Emergent literacy: Writing and reading* (pp. 173–205). Norwood, NJ: Ablex.

Theoharis, J. (2013). *The rebellious life of Mrs. Rosa Parks.* Boston: Beacon.

Tillman, L. C. (2004). African American parent involvement in the post-*Brown* era: Facilitating the academic achievement of African American students. *Journal of School Public Relations, 25*(2), 161–176.

Tuan, Y-F. (1979). Space and place: Humanistic perspective. In S. Gale & G. Olsson (Eds.), *Philosophy in geography* (pp. 387–427). New York: Springer.

United States Department of Education. (1987). *What works: Research about teaching and learning* (2nd ed.). Washington, DC: U.S. Government Printing Office.

Valdés, G. (1996). *Con respeto: Bridging the distances between culturally diverse families and schools: An ethnographic portrait.* New York: Teachers College Press.

Wacquant, L. J. (1995). The ghetto, the state, and the New Capitalist economy. In P. Kasinitz (Ed.), *Metropolis: Center and symbol of our times* (pp. 418–449). New York: New York University Press.

Walker, V. S. (1996). *The highest potential: An African American school community in the segregated south.* Chapel Hill: University of North Carolina Press.

Warlick, J. (2011). Have South Bend's schools become resegregated? Racial trends in the SBCSC since school year 1996–97. Unpublished manuscript. South Bend, IN.

Warren, M. (2005). Communities and schools: A new view of urban education reform. *Harvard Educational Review, 75*(2), 133–172.

Warren, M., Hong, S., Rubin, C., & Uy, P. (2009). Beyond the bake sale: A community-based relational approach to parent engagement in schools. *Teachers College Record, 111*(9), 2209–2254.

Watkins, W. (Ed.). (2012). *The assault on public education. Confronting the politics of corporate reform.* New York: Teachers College Press.

Watson, D. (2011). What do you mean when you say urban? Speaking honestly about race and students. *Rethinking Schools, 26*(1). Available at http://www.rethinkingschools.org/archive/26_01/26_01_watson.shtml

Weiss, H., Bouffard, S., Bridglall, B., & Gordon, E. (2009). Reframing family involvement in education: Supporting families to support educational equity. Available at http://www.equitycampaign.org/i/a/document/12018_equitymattersvol5_web.pdf

Wilson, W. J. (1987). *The truly disadvantaged.* Chicago: University of Chicago Press.

Wilson, W. J. (1996). *When work disappears: The world of the new urban poor.* New York: Vintage.

Winn, M., & Behizadeh, N. (2011). The right to be literate: Literacy, education, and the school-to-prison pipeline. *Review of Educational Research, 35*(1). Available at http://rre.aera.net

Wright, R. (2004). The language: Exploring the hidden meanings in *Plessy* and *Brown.* In J. Anderson & D. Byrne (Eds.), *The unfinished agenda of* Brown v. Board of Education (pp. 97–106). New York: John Wiley & Sons.

Woodson, C. (2012). *The mis-education of the Negro.* New York: Tribeca Books.

Yosso, T. J. (2005). Whose culture has capital? A critical race theory discussion of community cultural wealth. *Race, Ethnicity, and Education, 8*(1), 69–91.

Index

About the Author

Stuart Greene is associate professor of English with a joint appointment in the department of Africana Studies at the University of Notre Dame. His research has focused on the intersections of race, poverty, and achievement in public schools. This work has led to the publication of his coedited volume with Dawn Abt-Perkins, _Making Race Visible: Literacy Research for Racial Understanding_ (Teachers College Press, 2003), for which he won the National Council of Teachers of English Richard A. Meade Award in 2005. He also edited _Literacy as a Civil Right_ (2008) and coedited _Bedtime Stories and Book Reports: Connecting Parent Involvement and Family_ (Teachers College Press, 2010) with Cathy Compton-Lilly.